You're More Than What Meets the Eye: The Independent
Woman's Guide to Becoming Wifely Material
© 2012 by Antoinette Smith. All rights reserved.

Published by Freedom Stream in the United States of America.

ISBN 13: 978-0-9857304-1-3
ISBN 10: 0-9857304-1-2

All rights reserved. The reproduction, transmission or utilization of this work in whole or in part in any form by any electronic, mechanical or other means, now known or hereafter invented, including xerography, photocopying and recording, or in any information storage or retrieval system, is forbidden without written permission. For written permission, please contact Freedom Stream, 1421 SW 107th Avenue, Ste. 230, Miami, FL 33174 U.S.A.

Names and identifying characteristics of certain individuals in this book have been changed in order to protect their privacy.

Scripture taken from the NEW AMERICAN STANDARD BIBLE®, Copyright ©1960, 1962,1963,1968,1971,1972,1973,1975,1977,1995 by The Lockman Foundation. Used by permission.

www.YoureMore.com

Copy Editor: E. Claudette Freeman/E. Claudette Freeman Literary Services
Cover Design: Christoper Thomas of Chris Thomas Graphics
Illustrator: Shauntia A. Lynch a/k/a Shaunie
Interior Design: Brandi K. Etheredge

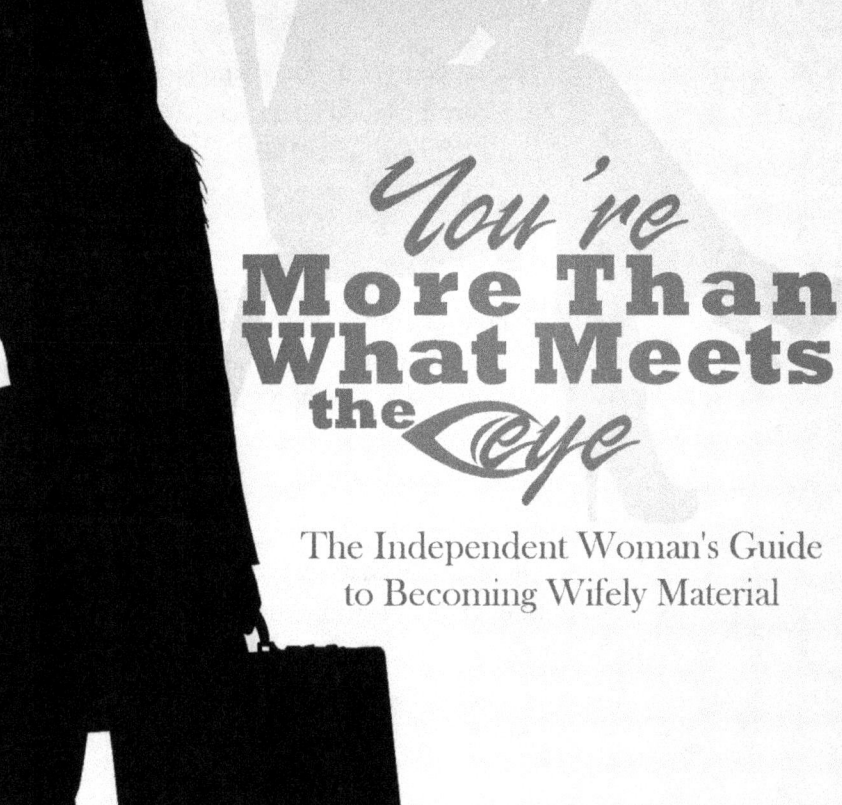

You're More Than What Meets the eye

The Independent Woman's Guide to Becoming Wifely Material

Dr. Antoinette Smith

Do not be misled: "Bad company
corrupts good character."
Corinthians 15:33

He who finds a wife finds what is good
and receives favor from the Lord.
Proverbs 18:22

A wife of noble character who can find?
She is worth far more than rubies.
Her husband has full confidence in her
and lacks nothing of value.
She brings him good, not harm,
all the days of her life.
Proverbs 31:10-12

Table Of Contents

Acknowledgements 7

Prelude 8

Section One:
Through An Independent Woman's Eyes And What We See 12
    Introduction 13
    An Independent Woman Prays For Her Husband 17
    The Real Beginning of Love…My Story 19
    My Education Finally Pays Off 23
    Your Genre of Music = Your Feelings 25
    Lights, Camera, Action 28

Section Two:
Oh, The Things We Tell Ourselves! 30
    Introduction 31
    What's Wrong with Being Too Independent? 32
    I Am Unmarried by Choice! 34
    But Men Are a Waste of Time! 37
    Men Cannot Be Trusted, Right? 40
    Marriage and Men Are Too Difficult 44
    What if He's the Opposite of Me? 47
    My Heritage Teaches Me to Be Strong! 50
    I Cannot Help Myself 54
    What's the Big Deal About Marriage? 57
    Perhaps Marriage is Not For Me… 60

    Section Three:
Analyzing Negative Behavior 63
Introduction 64
    How Did I Get Here? 65
    It's All About Me 68
    If You are Near a Mirror, Go Stand There 71
    Going Behind the Scenes 74
    Paradigm-Preserving Models of a Relationship—The Don'ts 77
    Listen to Your Internal/Hidden Layer 86
    Paradigm-Preserving Mindset—A Deeper Look 89
    Paradigm-Shifting to Paradigm-Modifying 93

Section Four:
Putting The Transition Into Motion 98
    Introduction 99
    So How Do I Shift? 100
    The Spring Cleaning Approach 103
    Your Friends and Yes, Your Mother 108
    I am From Missouri, the Show-Me State 114
    How to Behave During the Paradigm Shift (aka "The Wilderness") 117

Section Five:
From The Wilderness To Being Even More Transparent 123
    Introduction 124
    What Do I Have to Sacrifice? 125
    Where Do I Start? 128
    But I Fear Exposing the Real Me 130
    Your Cry for Help 134
    Remain Focused Throughout the Process 136
    What Can I Do About My Toughest Moments in the Wilderness? 137
    Finally, a Road Map to Guide Me Into Becoming Marriage Material ...140
    What Should I Expect From Others During My Transition? 146
    When Do I Apologize? 148
    Transition Like a Backstroke 150
    How Do I Get Out of The Wilderness? 153
    How Do I Get Out of The Wilderness—There's More? 156

Epilogue 160

About The Author 163

Acknowledgements

To My Dearest Jonathan: When I think about the love you have for me and our family and when I think about the man you are, I know that I am highly favored by God. You are everything that I want and need in a man. I want to thank you for experiencing the rough seasons with me and for your steadfastness during my toughest moments. Thank you for encouraging me, praying for me, being my best friend, and reassuring me of your love. You are my dream come true.

To My Dear Daughters: It is through your love, smiles, and experiences that I keep moving forward. You teach me so much each day. I am thankful for our mother/daughter bond. Jaleesa and Shauntia, the moments we share are enduring, and I am proud of the ladies you have become. Thanks for riding the waves and providing unconditional, unstoppable love. Tyra and Christina, your beautiful smiles and warm eyes remind me that life is great. God knew that I needed you in my life. Thank you for loving me each day and expressing your support in everything that I do.

I also want to acknowledge my parents, Lee and Betty, for setting the example in the areas of commitment, dedication, forgiveness, love, family, transition, marriage, and prayer. Mom, thank you for being a great role model.

To my sisters, Maleka and Leenette: Your undying love, encouragement, and support are amazing. Thanks for leaning on me and allowing me to lean on you.

To my team of pastors: Wayne Lomax, Kevin Taylor, and Russell St. Bernard, thank you for always being available to provide guidance and encouragement. Pastor Lomax, thank you for ministering and mentoring me and encouraging men to be great leaders, husbands, and dads. Pastor Taylor, thank you for your insight, motivation, and invaluable guidance while I wrote this book. Pastor Russ, thank you for telling me everything that I needed to know to get this book published.

To my wonderful friends: Lisa, Marlene, and Vivian. Thank you for always being available. Everyone needs friends like you. Your wisdom has helped me tremendously through my transitioning process to becoming wifely material.

There are many names unmentioned. I am thankful to everyone who contributed, both directly and indirectly, to the success of this book. Thank you.

To My Father – The Almighty God: Thank You! Thank You! Thank You! When I think about how far you have brought me and how much you have taught me, my soul cries out, Hallelujah!

Prelude

The shelves of prominent bookstores and online book venues are saturated with titles that promote how a woman should behave in order to attract a man or how to know whether or not he is into her. Other titles give advice on how to be a strong, assertive woman who can write her own ticket when it comes to whom and what she wants in life. Yet there is something missing on those shelves for women like me—strong, professional, determined, financially-sound, ambitious women—who need to shift our mindsets if we want to be considered great marriage partners. There is nothing among this bevy of titles to help these women understand that they leave much to be desired when it comes to being marriage material. The lessons here are for the benefit of my fellow independent sisters from information that I have discovered during the life teachings I have experienced.

When I began my journey, I did not fully comprehend all that it took to be a wife. Prior to my transition, I was pretty self-absorbed and spoiled. I was so proud of being a financially-stable, independent, career-focused woman that I did not find it necessary to prioritize a relationship—at least not to the extent that I prioritized my education and career. As a matter of fact, I viewed married women as people skilled at dumbing down and being more tolerant of men. In other words, I assumed that they presented themselves as less than capable, less intelligent, and somewhat passive. I also thought married women lacked independence. To me, a woman who lacked independence had opted to lose herself for the sake of marriage.

I have learned that my views about married women are far from true. An independent woman is what most men want—but not an independent woman according to society's definition. You can actually spot a socially-defined independent, anti-marriage woman a mile away. This type of independent woman walks with a confidence ignited primarily by her own single-handed, Superwoman achievements and accomplishments. She is woman; hear her ROAR! She knows her self-worth and uses it to her advantage to strategically demonstrate her worth through selected channels and by her own free will. She is happy in many areas and excited that she does not have to ask or depend on a man for anything. She lives on her own island and controls who docks there while enjoying the fruit of her success. She rarely allows anyone to take full or partial control, particularly if she or someone close to her is impacted by the decisions that person will make. It is easy to understand why a man would not be happy with this particular kind of independent woman as his wife.

Men are not scared of independent women. However, the independent woman I just described is too much of a challenge for the long haul, even for a man who enjoys invigorating challenges. Far too often, the ROARING INDEPENDENT woman will roar even in moments when a purr is more effective. She must be right. She must have the first and final say. She must control everything, even when it comes to small things. Men are not afraid of a very specific kind of independent woman; in fact, they embrace them. They want the kind of independent woman who allows a man to be the leader he is designed to be. "Oh my," I hear you screaming, "If he is a man, then he should be the man. Why do I have to allow him to be?" It really is not a matter of allowing or letting him be a man; it is a matter of you not moving into the role ahead of him.

A man wants a strong woman who relies on him while trusting in his ability to lead. He longs for the ambitious woman who understands his challenges, vulnerabilities, and needs. She does not hold failure over his head. Men want to come home and be embraced by a woman who is not going to be competitive, strong-willed, and argumentative simply because she is strong, independent, and capable. Many men expend their workday dealing with THAT woman, so can you imagine the distress presented when he comes home to one? He spends the day on the competitive edge in a battle of wills trying not to say anything disrespectful to women and making strides to applaud his female co-workers' success while trying to reach his own goals. After a day like this, he enters the doors to his castle and his refuge only to begin the same battle all over again. If the shoe were on the other foot, we certainly would not appreciate it. It strokes a man's ego to have an independent woman who says and shows him that "I believe in you, I trust you with me and us, I need you, and I want you."

If you are truly an independent woman, the very nature of your behavior and your career demonstrates your ability to achieve without a man. But why show that demeanor one hundred percent of the time, particularly when there is a better way? I am a convert to that better way. I now understand, due to many trials and failures, that Ms. Got-It-Working-Fiercely in the business world does not have to be that same person at home. My desire is to encourage other career-focused, powerful, take-charge, in-control women to consider working toward a new point of balance and to welcome re-adjustment in some (or most) of the attitudes and behaviors that come with being a fierce diva or independent woman.

Thoughts to Ponder

On a scale of 1 to 10, how independent are you?
Are you the decision-maker or leader in most of your relationships?

On a scale of 1 to 10, how easy is it for you to simply sit back and let a man make all the decisions on a date, when traveling, or when selecting a restaurant?

Has anyone ever told you that you are too controlling? If yes, what do you believe they meant?

Prelude

Section One
Through An Independent Woman's Eyes and What We See

Introduction

As I was penning this book, I was also enjoying one of the greatest pleasures of my life—my honeymoon with my new husband. We had been married about six days when we returned and I realized that I felt good. I was so proud and overjoyed, particularly because I had matured to a different and elevated level in relationships. I had, and was continuing to become, "wifely." I know that it was God's work that transformed my thoughts and behavior into what makes me who I am today and brought me to an understanding of my role as a wife, a mother, and a person in this journey.

I have gleaned a tremendous amount of wisdom regarding the stereotypical attitudes of women portrayed in the media. Through the diverse networks of women that I interact with, I have observed that many non-wifely characteristics exist across cultures. I have also gained valuable insight about how a woman should be: soft, pretty, passionate, supportive, a listener, a comforter, a lover, a best friend, a confidante, a follower, and a leader. I hope, like me, your eyes become open and your willingness to change allows you to transform yourself and, therefore, your future (or current) husband, your marriage, your family, and the world.

Perhaps you tried everything you could in the past (to become more wifely). I am sure you did, but was it done the right way and with the right mindset? Your intentions had nothing to do with the results. In other words, you may have intended to marry, but if you did not place yourself into training, your intentions alone did not help you accomplish your goal.

This time around, you have to embrace the standards of being a wife. You must accept the challenge and walk into the light of what you believe about yourself. Embody wifely behavior with a passion. If you do not gain a husband, press forward - you have nothing to lose but a lot to gain. You gain the understanding that whatever intrinsic modifications you make increase the quality of who you are first and are then passed over to the husband who will come along.

As a woman, you must continue to grow and learn. You must have expectations indicative of a great marriage and a family that prospers as a result of your growth. You must acknowledge your fears, faults, and weaknesses. You must learn to appreciate what matters most in life. You must be able to read these words looking for something to open your eyes. If you are in denial about why you are not in a relationship or point your finger at everyone else, you might want to read this book a little later in life. If you are ready for self-awareness and reflection, this book is for you. This book is for you if you would like to settle down someday but may not know how to open up enough to be ready for marriage. This book provides insight and methods on how you can take time to get to know who you really are so you can avoid your own pitfalls and the pitfalls of marriage.

Becoming marriage material is a process; before you can know what you will and will not accept, you have to understand who you are now and how to reveal the better you. You have to be methodical throughout this process and plan to display marriage-like behavior in every applicable area of your life. When you really want something, you have to plan to get it. If marriage is in your future, you have to plan to be married happily-ever-after. My husband spoils me and I know to never take him or our marriage for granted. The best contribution I can make to our marriage is being the best me. Given that we are now one, the best me should bring about the best in him. So, let me help you work on being the best you.

How do you know if you are over or under analyzing? How do you know if you are marriage material? Who are your marriage material role models? Did you have good or bad examples of what it takes to be a wife? This book helps you address these questions.

Do not block your blessings. Let the man be the man. Our independence can make it difficult for us to simply ride in the passenger seat of a good man's life without concern about where we are going, the route we are taking, and the time it will take to arrive.

No one is perfect. When you become married, you will continue to be a work-in-progress. But you should do what it takes to start from a good place. If you have witnessed bad marriages, then allow my insight to be your guide.

Thoughts to Ponder

Do you believe you can be passionate about being a wife?

Have you ever taken a man for granted?

What is your area of expertise? Do you think you could also become an expert in the area of being a good wife?

Do you have what it takes to be a good wife? Please explain.

Who has been your good wife role model?

An Independent Woman Prays For Her Husband

Dear Lord,

I desire a husband. Please bring the right individual into my life. Dear Lord, I pray that he is gentle, kind, supportive, a Godly man, my friend, my protector, strong, manly, a leader, has a home, and has two children. I pray that he understands that I am not perfect and that you are still working on me. I pray that he accepts me with all my faults and makes me a better person. I pray that I will grow and be happy as a result of being his wife.

Lord, you know my ways, my thoughts, my strengths, and my weaknesses. Thus, please help me rely completely on you for bringing the right person into my life. I pray that I can be all the things to him that you would want of me to be. Lord, I know you do not limit what I can ask for in my prayers, thus I pour my heart out to you knowing that you will supply all my needs and give me what you want me to have. Prepare me, Lord, from head to toe, give me wisdom in identifying the man you send to me. I love you, Lord, and you are the only one I can come to for this request.

Your Child,
Antoinette

Thoughts to Ponder

Do you believe in prayer? If so, what do you pray about? Have your prayers been answered?

Do you believe in praying for a husband?

What are you praying for in a husband? What are you seeking God's help for in becoming a wife?

The Real Beginning of Love... My Story

Throughout all of my previous relationships, I felt that I was the reward. I believed and behaved like I was the most valuable person in the relationship and, therefore, had options in life and in men. Clearly, I thought, I could not be wrong in living out this mindset. It was a powerful picture painted of me by those closest to me. In each image I was told that I was educated, a great catch, and an attractive woman. All of this ultra-positive reinforcement and applause told me I was the ultimate trophy.

If we are not careful, these thoughts that are meant to be powerful and uplifting can become prideful and self-stimulating body armor. We become accustomed to wearing this armor that allows us to bathe in uplifting words while simultaneously protecting our most sensitive areas, hiding our fears, and obscuring our best character. This body armor prevents people from seeing the true us. Calling all women… will the real you please stand up?!?

I was not wise enough to seek candid advice. During my early years, although I was a wife, I was not ready to be a wife. It took me almost a decade to figure out why. I am thankful that I gained insight from my blindness and lack of wisdom so I could overcome my shortcomings and bounce back.

Initially, while I understood the power of prayer and would pray for and about everything, I never prayed for a husband. I prayed for everything but a husband. I recall focusing my prayers on sustaining abstinence, excelling in my career, business and finances, safeguarding my children, and being able to connect with and hear from God. I actively participated in my church's prayer line to collectively pray for others, our families, and ourselves. God answered prayers for me and others on the call. Then suddenly in 2007 the revelation came—just like I needed financial prosperity, I also needed a man. Yes, I said that—I needed a man. I needed my man!

I called the prayer line as always, but this time something in me said, "Make your request for a husband known to God." That was my prayer request on that night: "God send me a husband." Just speaking those words and boldly releasing my request lifted what felt like a huge burden. It was a courageous move. During my one-on-one prayer time with God, I asked for the right husband and for help in preparing myself for the right man. I asked God to give me wisdom and peace. I talked to God, letting Him know that I had full confidence that He would send the man I needed in my life. Part of me felt like this was an eleventh hour prayer request; after all, I had two children, an outstanding career, and I had been married once before. From a tangible possessions perspective, I had all that a woman could possibly want, even men who were just a phone call away and a few men trying to disguise themselves as "The One." Why did it take me so long to understand that if God answered all of my other prayers, He would answer this one too? Why did I comfortably allow my two daughters to grow alongside me and not give them insight on the skills necessary to get married and maintain a marriage? Why was my focus less on marriage preparation than on other goals? I knew that I had to go through a process, especially if I wanted to be a great wife, but someone should have said, "While you can find someone who will marry you, unfortunately you are not ready to be a wife. In all your greatness, in all your achievements, in all your confidence, you are not ready to be the best wife." When I began to open myself up to divine correction and instructions for change and then began to transition, married individuals began to say, "You will make a great wife someday." Strangers, friends, and family members began to speak these words to me, and it confirmed that I was rebounding from my shortcomings. It was, as the saying goes, "better late than never."

While I wish I had the wisdom years ago to understand the power of prayer as it relates to desiring a husband, the moment I opened up to God I benefitted. So many great things happened to me that transitioned my spiritual understanding of what it means to be a great person and what it means to be a wife. I do not seek to preach to you or thump you over the head with Biblical scriptures, but one of the most significant teachings on what a wife should be is found in the Bible book of Proverbs, Chapter 31. It speaks about a wife—not a girlfriend, a boo, a sweet thing or a sugar mama—but a wife. Bishop T. D. Jakes, founding pastor of The Potter's House in Dallas, Texas, has often said in his teachings that a wife is a wife before she is married. This woman is smart; makes great business decisions; and manages her children, and her home—while making her husband look good. Bishop Jakes taught she could not have stepped into that role if she had not been prepared for it. She has prepared herself and taken on the position of a wife in her life, so she simply becomes that for the man designed to be her husband, which is what I believe Proverbs 31 teaches. Was my prayer that night an invitation to move into my time of wifely preparation? If it was, then I had to conduct some self-assessment. Slowly my eyes began to open to some hard truths about myself. One of those initial revelations was that during my first marriage and previous relationships I was neither the best wife nor was I the best person. You see, as I prayed for things such as the needs of others; blessings for others; removal of any signs of anger and pride; an increase in my patience; and being a better mom, sister, professor, and daughter, God had to show me what I had to deal with in me to become what I was praying for.

If you are anything close to what I used to be, you have a truckload of confidence and believe that any man is lucky to have you. After gaining wisdom that this was not the case, I apologized to all the guys who came my way before I stood in front of that mirror and took a long hard look at what I portrayed. I was nowhere close to wifely. My mindset and my actions said, "We can do well together, but you are very fortunate to find a woman of my caliber. Your job is to spoil me." Yep, I was a self-centered, overconfident, spoiled, entitled, dreamer with super high expectations. My concept was "Name it, I have it, so what are you coming to the table with? Is it comparable or better than what I have?" I have grown and moved far from this mindset, which has benefitted everyone—my husband, family, friends, and our contacts.

Thoughts to Ponder

What is your love story?

Do your mentees and family members benefit from your love stories? If so, how?

Who should you call and apologize to because of your behavior in a past relationship?

My Education Finally Pays Off

My true intelligence shines in the matriculation of knowing how to love a man, maintain balance in my career and family, and in understanding and continuously evaluating my core of true happiness. Not many things are more challenging than being wifely material. Surely since I consider myself to be all that, I should be able to master this high calling, right? Well, I am doing it, baby, day-by-day, with my eyes, mind, and spirit open to change. I am excited about being well-equipped and upgraded for what lies ahead. My husband is wonderfully made. My family will continue to be blessed for generations to come because of who and where we are today and my decision to change.

This is the roadmap to preparing yourself to be a wife. Your immaturity, lack of preparation, lack of commitment to prepare, and your lack of growth will begin to surface. Allow it all to do just that so you can engage the opportunities to clean up some intrinsic things and not carry the baggage from those things further into your life and your relationships. I want you to arrive at being an equipped and prepared, ready-to-be wife. In this capacity, you will be like the wife I mentioned in Proverbs 31—a wife who is able to maintain the splendor, the wonder, and the fullness of a relationship. In order for wisdom to occur in the matrimonial process, you must take deliberate steps to focus on your shortcomings and transform yourself into a better you. You must reveal the hidden layers so that you and others can see the true you.

Thoughts to Ponder

What layers have you hidden from yourself? Why?

What layers have your hidden from others? Why?

Your Genre of Music = Your Feelings

I have a friend who works as a radio personality. He says people—often the same people—make several song requests throughout the night and he knows what they are experiencing at that very moment from the selection of songs they choose. I recall playing a group of albums almost on a daily basis for years. In this group of albums was R & B artist R. Kelly's "Bump N Grind," along with music from 12-Play, Destiny's Child, and TLC. Mary J. Blige, the Queen of Hip Hop, was a particular favorite of mine. Her songs "My Life," "Mary," "Share My World," "What's the 411," "No More Drama," and her album *The Breakthrough* were frequently on my playlist. My favorite song from *The Breakthrough* album was one called "Be Without You." During my R. Kelly season, life was about drinks, fun, and parties (in moderation, of course.) If I was doing well in school and on the job, my weekends were defined by hanging out with my other sexy friends or painting the town solo, flirting and dancing. At one time, I repeatedly listened to the smooth vocals of Toni Braxton, specifically her album *Secrets*. I enjoyed how she poured her heart out in these stories about a woman hurt by someone she loved while at the same time being sexy and aware of her state of confusion and looking for a solution. Now I understand that was how I viewed relationships. While I was not experiencing the lyrics on the *Secrets* album, I understood and acknowledged what could happen to me and how I would potentially feel if those situations occurred in my life. My huge breakthrough songs were undoubtedly "No More Drama" and "Be Without You." Excuse me, you say? What? I went from believing I lived in a drama-free zone to singing songs that proclaimed that I was vulnerable, had insecurities, and, worst of all, could not be without a man.

My DJ friend is right. Songs help us understand our passions, motivations, and beliefs. Our favorite songs have lyrics that speak to us and can help us understand our perceptions about what we are currently experiencing or embracing. My husband would often sing R & B artist Ne-Yo's "Miss Independent" to and about me after we initially met. He would say with a beautiful smile on his face, "Baby, I love this song because it reminds me of you. I like an independent woman."

I can still see him tapping his fingers on the steering wheel and moving his upper body as he sang that tune. When I met him, I had already realized that a transition was needed, and so I was not so happy knowing this was the song that made him smile about me. Two years prior to meeting him, it would not have been a problem. I probably would have proudly affirmed the lyrics myself. However, I wanted to say to him that the song was not what I was about or who I wanted to be. I was completely confused. Perhaps "Miss Independent" was a good image for a woman who wanted to become a wife. Perhaps I should be excited about such a positive song reminding him of me. Yet, the song was exactly what I was trying to minimize. Yes, I lived in an upscale neighborhood in South Florida. Yes, I had my Ph.D. Yes, I looked well put together. Yes, I was a fun person to be around. However, I also knew a "boss" image contradicted what I wanted to be in a relationship. I had a desire to be humble, dependent on, and interdependent with a man. I wanted to tell him I had fears, insecurities, and needs. I wanted to tell him I did not want to be the boss and that I wanted a man who could take care of me—one who I could respect and love, who I could need and lean on. I wanted to turn off my leadership, boss-mentality when I was not at work and just relax fearlessly in his strong arms. He seemed so happy when he was singing that song. I did not want to burst his bubble. I had also learned that there is a right time for everything, and I understood the importance of letting others flow in their energy. My new understanding allowed me to allow him to have fun in his view of his lady as an independent woman. It reflected as much about where he was in his life as I was in my development. His singing that song took me back to a chapter of my life that I was not particularly proud of. Every time his voice wrapped around the lyrics—and they were playing the song a lot on the radio at the time—it reminded me of so many things that I once valued improperly that separated me from being a future wife. I was so thankful when he stopped singing that song and went on to more romantic, loving, and passionate ones.

I have to admit, I still listen closely to determine if his latest tunes symbolize how he is feeling about me and our life together.

So what is your song saying about you? Is it saying it's time to change so love can come in? Is it saying let it go and let love have its way? Or is your song still telling you that you are all that and a bag of chips? I believe that you are all that and so much more. However, I also believe that there is more to all of us than meets the eye. As women, we have bought into the hype of being great, powerful, independent, wise, and smarter than men. We have also taken great stock in being leaders, conquerors, and multi-taskers armed with a long list of accolades. From the very beginning, we are told that boys develop at a slower rate than girls, which eggs us on in the thought that we move faster and potentially do more sooner than men. We enjoy popular slogans, such as "Girl Power!" "Girls Rule!" and "Girls Kick Butt!" We are very capable of tooting our own horns. However, the acceptance of these accolades is a double-edged sword. One edge presents an accurate reflection of our true potential. The other edge reveals limitations within the mindset that keep many wonderful, attractive, and well-educated women unmarried.

Thoughts to Ponder

What type of music do you listen to now?

What type of music did you listen to five years ago?

Consider how your choice of music relates to what is happening in your life. What is revealed through this consideration?

What songs can you listen to that highlight positive relationships?

If you are in a relationship, what music does your mate listen to? Could it be a reflection of how he feels about the relationship? Have you asked him?

Lights, Camera, Action

Hollywood does a great job of promoting the highly independent, successful, single woman. We no longer see the strength of family as once portrayed in *Leave It To Beaver*, *The Cosby Show*, or even *The Jeffersons*. Regardless of the socio-economic status of the respective television families in different eras, we saw strong marriages featuring couples that worked through the hard times and represented a thriving family unit. In the 60s and 70s, television families ate dinner together, stayed together, and had happy marriages. Shows challenged us to want to be the wife (or husband) who reflected the core values essential to family. This changed over time. The images bombarding television screens by the mid-2000s seemed to support the paradigm-preserving mentality that career is so important that you really do not have time for a relationship or the limitations of a man.

We do not see the earlier positive images of marriage in today's reality shows; very few are family-oriented. As women, Hollywood gives us little inspiration to be a spouse with a wonderful family. They feed us highly successful women who lead corporations, are entrepreneurs, and are embroiled in trivial drama that is entertainment banter. It is very easy for these images to become our motivation and ideology. Thus, if we had to choose from the options provided by Hollywood, most of us would want to be the highly independent, single, and successful woman portrayed in top-rated shows. This is especially true when all we see as our option is the single mother filled with drama.

Thoughts to Ponder

What TV shows do you watch?

Which radio stations do you listen to?

How does what you see on TV and hear on the radio impact your thoughts about relationships? Please explain.

Section Two

Oh, the Things We Tell Ourselves!

Introduction

Many single and divorced women have a long list of reasons why marriage is not for them and should be avoided, why it is no longer vital or necessary, or why it is a male-centered system. We hide behind these strong walls of reasons, excuses, and determinations and fail to embrace the power of being a wife. Can we just call out these banners that hang on the walls we hide behind and then knock down the walls?

What's Wrong with Being Too Independent?

A woman's mind can be programmed through various statements and demonstrations like "You can do it without a man." Accordingly, every form of success instilled in a woman is that as an independent woman, she can achieve. The problem with the independent mindset and programming, however, is that The Creator did not design us to think that way. Society, our upbringing, and our experiences created that gross misconception. This is where the tension for most women comes in the area of wanting a good man but not doing what it takes to attract a good man. Take your eyes out of the magazines, turn the channel away from those demeaning and scripted reality shows, turn off the banter on radio talk shows, and focus on the husband who you want to love. When that focus is clear, identify and make the adjustments within to bring him to your arms.

Thoughts to Ponder

Why do you feel a need to be independent?

How has your level of independence interfered with your relationships?

Do you feel you have to dumb yourself down for a man? Please explain.

Section Two

I Am Unmarried by Choice!

When I hear a woman cast this vision of non-marriage in her life, I know immediately that as long as she maintains this vision and gives it light (meaning she shares it openly and with authority with others), her vision shall come true. I often hear women state that they are unmarried by choice. My perception of this proclamation is that she is casting a vision of incompleteness. In other words, she has decided not to prepare herself for marriage. Typically, a positive correlation exists between our choices and our outcomes. Most of us begin to stereotype individuals given what we know, see, or assume about them and their pattern of choices.

My paradigm-preserving mindset told me I was single by choice, so all of my judgments and decisions fit within my "single-by-choice" mindset. The clothes I purchased, the locations I visited, the discussions I had with family members, my favorite television shows, my career choices, my music, and the advice I would seek all fit within the frame of my single-headed mindset. I never asked anyone questions like "What would it take for me to become a great wife?" or "What are some beliefs or behaviors that you think I need to release in order to be a great wife?" While I never asked these questions, I would ask for advice on promotions, relocating, and training in addition to all the pertinent questions necessary to help me shatter the proverbial glass ceiling. It was all a sham!

When I began to shift my mindset, I immediately knew that I was, in fact, single by choice. Unconsciously, I replayed thoughts similar to "If the right guy comes along…" "When I am ready, if ever I am ready, I will open myself up to a husband," "I can never deal with what most married women deal with," "As long as I am single, I only have to be concerned about me and my girls," and finally "I enjoy having my freedom." Once I became aware that I was using the best years of my life to speak and bring these crippling affirmations to the forefront, I toyed with the thought of being able to have the best of both worlds. I thought it would be great to have the freedom to be a better me while also having the freedom to love, nurture, and have sex with my husband as much as my heart desired. I was quite scared that one of these thoughts would overpower the other. In other words, I did not want to get so wrapped up into shaping myself into becoming a wife that I allowed my career to suffer. Once I conquered that fear, I made a conscious decision to marry a wonderful man one day. Your mind is very powerful, so if you continue to believe you are unmarried by choice, the evidence before you will likely align within this paradigm-preserving mindset.

Thoughts to Ponder

Have you concluded that you will never get married? Please explain.

Have you ever told yourself or heard someone say that they were not cut out to be married? What are your thoughts about these statements?

Why do you believe people count themselves out when it comes to marriage?

But Men Are a Waste of Time!

I will admit it; some men are a waste of time, but not all men. Some single women have proudly proclaimed variations of the following reasons as to why they are unmarried. I would have to dumb myself down. I would rather be by myself than settle for just anything. I can do bad all by myself! He has to meet all of the requirements on my list. I'll wait until my children leave the house. I am too busy for a relationship! God made me to be single. Lesbianism is an option. All men cheat! Men are stressful and too sensitive! I want to be financially stable first.

Now imagine someone making these statements about you. It does not sit well with you, does it? Can you imagine sharing your entire life with someone who feels negatively about you, your race, and your gender? No one can be happy under these conditions.

The way we process information is rooted in our mindset, which has been shaped by our experiences and practices. I hope I am providing you with food for thought and that you will absorb and apply all of the information I am giving you so you can transform into a wonderful and powerful wife. The first step is to move from a paradigm-preserving mindset to a paradigm-modifying mindset.

Who programmed our mindsets? I believe no one wants to live alone. I cannot imagine the average woman embracing the idea of growing old by herself.

It seems to me there would be times that she would feel empty, despite the home, the cars, the family, and the friends. It would sadden me to look around and see that I had everything I needed, except for a husband. I do believe I would continuously ask myself what is it about me that allowed me to gain so much materially yet no one to make a lifetime commitment with. At times, everything would seem so right, but at the same time a quiet moment would reveal that I was so empty. I have been around enough intelligent, affluent women to know that while they are smiling and joking on the outside, there is so much hurt inside. There is something not quite right within them, but it is easier to state that something is not quite right about him. Despite what you see and what the facts suggest, marriage can bring you joy and peace in ways that are impossible to achieve as a single woman. Marriage can be your greatest achievement, even when it brings rough seasons.

Thoughts to Ponder

Do you tend to speak more from a positive or a negative aspect about life?

What about marriage? Please explain.

Do you consider marriage an achievement? Please explain.

Section Two

Men Cannot Be Trusted, Right?

Women tend to have an issue with trust. However, please understand that trust does not have to be earned by anyone until they have personally given you a reason not to trust them. In other words, everyone you decide to court gets a clean slate of trust. They do not have to work to earn your trust, given they have done nothing to demonstrate they are untrustworthy. Further, no one is perfect, not even you, so you should not be in search of a perfect man. You cannot even put your complete trust in yourself to always do what is right, so why expect that of others? What you really want is a partner by your side who is committed to the relationship—someone who you can become one with and make it clear to all that your marriage is sacred. The two of you are in fact unified.

Is it possible that you may have hardships in the form of past adultery, arguments, and misplaced trust? Is it possible that your husband may cheat on you in the future? Absolutely. It is also possible that he will not. It is also likely that you will experience some form of hardship in a marriage. Yet, at the same time, I doubt you have had a successful career free from pain, surprises, and disappointments either. I doubt that you or your parents have raised children free of pain, surprises, missteps, heartbreak, and disappointment. So why hold a man to the requirements of not giving you challenges, disappointments, and failures? I also doubt that you are Ms. Perfect and that you will never cause your potential husband pain. Therefore, do not worry about something you cannot control. Here is a dialog I engaged in with a twice-divorced friend via text message about this very thing:

> **Friend:** Hello, I am not sure if I answered 1 of ur ques. The 1 that asked why I am not married. The true answer is that I haven't found anyone that I can trust to be true to me until death and that I can be proud of as my spouse. I know, I thought about that because someone else asked me that ques.
>
> **Me:** That's what you told me. You r asking a lot, given that we are all imperfect people.
>
> **Friend:** You think that I am asking too much? Faithful, support, and a person u can respect?
>
> **Me:** Absolutely. We all want that, both men and women, but God is the only perfect person. U have to develop a relationship to minimize the risk of infidelity, but no one on this earth could guarantee that to u.
>
> **Friend:** That's true, why are some of us programmed to think that way?
>
> **Me:** Because u have great optimism, but not realism.
>
> **Friend:** Wow, perhaps it was the fairy tales? Cinderella, Rapunzel, Snow White and the others
>
> **Me:** Lol. Exactly. That does not exist for anyone. Watch the kind of men you pick and how you make them feel. Otherwise, you will be grandma all by yourself.
>
> **Friend:** Thanks, I will need 2 read ur book ☺
>
> **Me:** ☺ If I had my book 5 yrs ago, I would be close to perfect by now. LOL
>
> **Friend:** Me too… ☺

I do understand lack of trust and how it evolves. However, I have never allowed trust to be an issue for me. While I value trust, I also recognize, and then eliminate, perpetual trust violators from my environment. Within a marriage, though, I do not have such freedom, thank goodness. I remember having a conversation with a married friend during a moment of paranoia about being a wife. While I thought the moment of being afraid of a life commitment would never happen to me, the fear of marriage arrived and departed within approximately twenty-four hours. During this moment, which occurred within thirty days of getting married, I asked her a lot of questions. What if he cheats on me? What if I cannot handle what a marriage brings? What if I discover something about him later that I cannot live with? In hindsight, this was a hilarious moment. I am glad I have a friend who understood my moment and who also knew my desires and could relate to my feelings. In her kindest, wife-like voice, she said, "Antoinette, you cannot control that part of a husband. That is not your concern. You concern yourself with focusing on God. Now get back to the business of being Mrs. Smith!"

My paranoid moment was simply short-term thinking and was not aligned with my goal of getting married, happily-ever-after, to the man of my dreams. When you want to completely trust someone, ask yourself can they completely trust you? If you are being honest with yourself, you should have answered no. Trust always involves a risk and it is hypocritical to expect one hundred percent trust from anyone. I do understand the pain of finding yourself with someone who reveals themselves as untrustworthy. When you lack trust in someone, particularly someone who has not given you reason to lack trust, you feel the need to conceal your fears, your past experiences, and the root cause for your lack of trust. It is important to realize that without the process of revealing, healing cannot occur. When you lack trust, a ticking time bomb is waiting to explode. No one wants to live their life trying to prove that they are trustworthy.

You should allow yourself to trust men, knowing that we are all imperfect individuals. Imperfect people can never expect perfection. Trust simply says, "I will do my best, but I have limitations." If we are honest, every person is capable of disappointing us, falling short of our expectations, and sinning. Whenever there is a risk, we can avoid the risk or mitigate the risk. I would suggest building your relationship on strong foundations and belief systems. By doing so, you minimize the risk of the relationship being impacted by negative behaviors. The same way you protect your vehicle and home from the risk of theft or vandalism, you need to do the same for your relationships.

Thoughts to Ponder

On a scale of 1 to 10, how perfect are you?

Have you ever lied to anyone? Did they know? Did they forgive you?
Do you find men trustworthy? Why or why not?

How has trust affected your views about relationships?

Marriage and Men Are Too Difficult

Yes, both can be difficult, more so if you have one of the following negative beliefs: that you are not cut out to be wifely material and were made to live and die unmarried; that men are incapable of being great husbands; that a marriage license is just a piece of paper that we do not need; or career definitely, marriage maybe. With such beliefs, we have the main driver of our thoughts. From our understanding of these drivers, we can then begin to change our beliefs and transition into a more powerful mindset shaped by positive affirming thoughts, such as "While I transition myself to wife-like material, my husband will also be in preparation." I believe that most women want to be married. The majority of us really do not want to be single but would rather marvel over the fact that our true love professed his love via a sky show with flashing lights displaying the words "Will You Marry Me?!" Because of this, I encourage you to always believe in the thought of being happily married so that when marriage comes you will be able to tell the story of how you made the choice to transition and how you got there by shifting your mindset. Happily married does not mean happily always.

During my season of vision-casting for my marriage, I took the first step of expecting a great marriage, as I continue to do so to this day. Before I initiated the second step of taking action, I painted a picture of happily married ever after!

There is some debate about the ability for anyone to be both married and happily married ever after. For me, I want to keep and believe in that vision—that happy, marriage, and ever after are eternal parts of my relationship. This means that my marriage will have bad and good days with the bigger goal that we achieve happily-ever-after once troubles settle. Marriage becomes the picture you paint. If you paint a picture of a marriage where you are at sixty-five percent sad and thirty-five percent happy, I can almost guarantee you that you will experience this proportion, or worse, in your marriage. I decided anything that upsets me in my marriage does not define me or my marriage and that all things will pass in time. If a difficulty occurs, once I get through it, I will continue on my path to happily-ever-after.

If you are unmarried, think about that one food or that one dessert that you wish you could overload on without any side effects such as gaining weight, getting cavities, or raising your cholesterol level. Mine is a huge slice of red velvet cake with buttermilk icing coupled with a cafe con leche. This is how I view my husband and my marriage. I had this vision of him being a delicious red velvet cake on a gold, diamond-trimmed platter before I married him. He and my marriage are the delicious treat that I desire to have the most. I realized that it allowed me to minimize all the minor issues that were brought to my attention. For instance, we can eat a bag of chips consisting of 280 calories per bag and never think twice about potato chip breath or weight gain. They seem so minor compared to the overall satisfaction of eating the chips. When you are courting, think of your future husband in this manner and do not sweat the small stuff. Think of him as your potential happily-ever-after. As you are overlooking the small things, simply focus on you and how you can improve your net worth.

Thoughts to Ponder

What picture do you paint for marriage?

How do your past experiences impact your image of marriage?

What have you achieved in life that has been easy to achieve?

What have you achieved in life that has been difficult to achieve?

Do you believe marriage should be easy to obtain and sustain? Please explain.

What if He's the Opposite of Me?

You have heard the saying that opposites attract. I remember one of my students asking me if my potential husband needed a Ph.D. While I simply laughed at the question without answering, I remember thinking, "Are you kidding me? Do you really think I would want someone who thinks and acts like me? NOT!" While my husband and I are on the same page when it comes to our core values and belief systems, we are quite opposite in several ways. However, since we became Mr. and Mrs. Smith, we seem to be more and more alike in our thinking processes than I realized. Differences become diluted when you respect and cherish what is really important and support each other. For example, let us assume that you are a person who is extremely rigid and who just happens to be dating a person who is extremely free-flowing. Ideally, the two of you would probably need each other to create the perfect balance. Without the other you would miss out on a lot in life because you are so rigid, while he is going to waste a lot in life because he is too free-flowing. If two opposite individuals can come together in a very symbiotic way, they can really complement each other. With balance between you, differences subside.

This is why I believe that opposites attract and it is not good to have a cloned mate. When you believe a person has to think like you, you are missing the purpose of life. Whenever we seek people who think and act like we do, we are not giving ourselves opportunities for expansion because everything we see in them fits within our paradigm-preserving mindset. In layman's terms, if you see everything in your world as blue, then all you see are blue people. You cannot expand your thought processes beyond the color blue with your mindset, even when other colors exist.

It is a mistake for you to want a husband who thinks and is too much like you. By cookie-cutting your future husband, you resist expansion, change, or self-observation. Therefore, I encourage you to keep an open mind and to never think that you have it all and know it all. Never believe that everything in the relationship has to be according to your belief system. What if your intended spouse has a belief system that they believe in and you have a belief system that you hold to be true? Do you just cut your ties and move forward, claiming you are not meant to be? What if you communicate your belief systems to each other, take the good out of both, and begin to redefine your belief system as a couple? As long as you stick with the "good," then it is a win-win situation. With or without a mate, ask yourself "How long have my belief systems been my belief systems?" When was the last software update you had in your beliefs? If your belief systems are not evolving, maturing, and improving, red flags should immediately go up. Nothing ventured, nothing gained.

Thoughts to Ponder

What would it be like to be with someone who thought like you?

What would it be like to be with someone who was opposite of you?

Does your ideal husband need to think and do everything like you? Please explain.

Section Two

My Heritage Teaches Me to Be Strong!

History tells us that African-Americans, Hispanics, and other multicultural women were forced to depend on themselves. Women learned very quickly to look out for themselves, fight their own battles, and take care of their children. This mindset of never depending on a man has perhaps reached your generation and continues to control your mindset; just keep in mind that your behavior may not be of your own making but the making of your heritage.

The U.S. Census Bureau, which collects general demographics in America, shows that there is a higher proportion of Black females who have never been married, divorced, or separated and a lower proportion of Black females who have been married than any other race. Another noticeable statistic is that the ratio of divorced or separated is almost equivalent across races. Studies continuously conclude that successful women are not getting married and that more children are born out of wedlock. No surprises here. For the most part, all races are less likely to find a man within their race who holds a higher degree. Trends signal that society needs to reorganize its life and priorities, especially women.

When I decided to pursue my Ph.D., I found myself surrounded by single men who either had a similar degree or were pursuing one. Within two years of being in this new environment, I received approximately three marriage proposals from individuals who were only my friends with no history of dating or sex. This was quite amazing to me. I could not help but notice how educated, good-hearted, and attractive they were, yet they felt their only hope was marrying me or outside their race. I witnessed several friends with higher degrees travel overseas to find wives. Each one of them proclaimed that it was difficult to find a good woman who could also be a good wife in the United States. I personally could not wrap my thoughts around this information. All I could see was that our network contained a sea of attractive, educated women. I was attending school in Florida and there was an entire campus of attractive women from around the country; most were on the slim side, with flawless skin, and always showed off their legs and feet by donning sexy high heels. As I continued to expand my horizons, I would hear the same thing over and over again from men of different walks of life in my family and social circles. I began to wonder what the problem was and why these seemly intelligent men believed there were no women who would make good wives available in America. Then it dawned on me that since it was a common theme from such a variety of men, perhaps there was some truth to the concept. Maybe the task of finding a good wife was not as easy as it appears.

The depiction of marriage is in a diminished state. So where does one find the reality of what it is intended to be and can be? It is more common to see a strong, independent woman than it is to see a loving and submissive wife. We generally reflect the environment from whence we come, so if the environment, according to the U.S. Census Bureau, substantiates that we are seeing less marriage and more strongly independent women leading families, then it stands to reason that is what is developing. The U.S. Census data further shows that females, especially African-American women, are surpassing Black males in academia matriculation. Women with higher education are likely to become more independent, and the men they would like to have become difficult to find. Therefore, these well-educated women have an anti-marriage form of independence that has reduced them in the lottery system. Here is what I am trying to say. The well-educated, employed man knows he is in demand. He knows his worth to a woman due to his level of matriculation, career position, and life experience. He knows that there are few men who can offer what he is offering. In other words, there are not many men who look like him and who have prepared themselves and developed themselves into rare commodities. Put yourself in this man's shoes and ask yourself if you would settle for a very combative, headstrong, highly independent woman when you realize all the options that exist and you know you are in high demand?

The way you treat a man will challenge some of your upbringing. However, the paradigm-preserving mindset has its limitations and pervasive consequences. If you are not willing to make a paradigm shift, then you are willing to follow the current trend. Nothing is easy in life. It is not easy getting a degree. It is not easy raising kids. It is not easy climbing the corporate ladder. Consequently, do not settle for easy in getting and maintaining a husband.

At the end of the day, a man wants a lovely, supportive, and endearing woman. He should not have to travel abroad or settle for corporate women who lack these qualities. Proverbs 31 talks about the rarity of a woman. Perhaps you have overcomplicated the matter with a list of demands you are seeking in a man. Ask yourself where this type of man exists in abundance. If you are looking for diamonds in the rough, this means you believe the diamond exists. You also must admit that it is a rarity to find a good diamond, and you must have a good eye to find the diamond cut for you. This is not the good eye that came with your paradigm-preserving vision but the good eye that came with your paradigm-modifying vision—the vision that gives you a new, clear, modified, and fresh look.

Thoughts to Ponder

Do you believe your heritage is controlling your thoughts? Please explain.

Does your family, in general, maintain healthy marriages? Please explain.

What skills would you have developed if you lived during a time when you never saw your wonderful husband again and you were left to take care of yourself? What skills would you teach your children and subsequent generations?

What general demographics do you fit in?

Do you fit the trends discussed in this chapter? If so, do you plan to remain within the trend?

Section Two

I Cannot Help Myself

Yes, you can. The way you behave and think in a relationship is a matter of choice. I recall a time when my husband and I were on our way to the airport. Heading up the departure ramp, I noticed that he was driving past our terminal entrance. I rushed to share this note of correction with him. He assured me that we needed to go to Terminal 3, not Terminal 1. When we got to Terminal 3, I could not wait to admit that I was right all along. I figured I would do it in a nice, clever way, which I did—or so I initially thought. However, my husband has a lot of wisdom, and while I tried to make the obvious error lighthearted, it was difficult for me to pull the wool over his eyes and the jab was received. Just like I made the choice to speak, I could have made the choice to allow my husband to identify his own mistake. I immediately knew I made the wrong choice in speaking up, especially considering I had more to gain by silence and nothing to gain by speaking out. More importantly, my choice to speak out was not driven out of a good place but out of a place of "I was right, you were wrong, and you should listen to me." Ladies, I am telling you to humble yourselves. Your marriage is not the boardroom and you will not get demoted or promoted for making your case in every situation. It is time to relax in the passenger seat and think about the other things that matter most to you.

In every scenario of a relationship, we have options in how we conduct ourselves. When we operate in a paradigm-preserving manner, we operate from a place where our thought processes are being manipulated by our environment, observations, teachings, and experiences. Our memory banks tend to hold much more than we think they do. The mind is very powerful. Just as we frequently clean out, defragment, and restore the hard drives on our computers, we must do the same for our minds. Often, we must clear everything out of there and, in essence, install a new hard drive or function from a brand new computer. When we fail to do this, we congest our thoughts and our lives with under-productive data, resulting in unaccomplished goals, poorly managed relationships, and data that does not fit our present or future endeavors, including marriage.

The point is clearer if we look at it this way. When you visit a website, your Internet browser remembers the website and will suggest websites and other information that fit within the pattern of previous searches. Similarly, when you encounter a situation in your relationship, you are likely to use the existing application (app) best equipped to handle that situation; maybe the app is automatically set and responds accordingly. Do you need to be equipped for the situation? Absolutely! Nevertheless, we can upgrade from a more defensive/protective armor gear to one that understands history and setbacks without letting them define us, thereby allowing new data to enter and process at a more positive, believing, and motivating speed.

When you use an app, you want it to come from your paradigm-*modifying* applications and not your paradigm-*preserving* applications. When you decide that you want to be married and make a continuous effort to be married, you need to begin working on your apps. They should state, "I can be nurturing and supportive," "I am kind and loving," and "Men would rather brag about having a good-looking, nurturing, and supportive woman rather than simply brag about her accomplishments." They deserve to have both.

Thoughts to Ponder

Have you ever initiated a debate with a man? What was the end result?

What will happen to you and the world if you could not prove your point of view or that you were right?

Do you have a soft/gentle side? When do you reveal this side of you?

What's the Big Deal About Marriage?

A marriage is not about the wedding, gifts, and honeymoon; it is about commitment, love, forgiveness and understanding, and compromising and sacrificing. Marriage requires us to change who we are, which can be a challenge.

Marriage upgrades your status. Before you go all bonkers, let me explain what I mean. I realize when I am in situations, such as talking to the service advisor at my Mercedes dealer, I often use the phrase "my husband." Oh, how sweet the sound of that! It actually tickles me. Since becoming a married woman, I truly enjoy using the phrase "my husband." It means that there are two heads. I am not in this alone. I have additional wisdom behind my decisions. I have protection.

I also notice that my colleagues and students perceive me differently. People put together facts about you based on the presence of a ring or no ring. I now know the extreme differences between the two. Since marriage, I am now able to experience a different level of respect than I did before—one that says you are Doctor *and* Mrs. Smith—even though prior to marriage, I believed my colleagues gave me the utmost respect. This new level of respect says you have the ability to manage this job and be a wife and mom. Wow! It is difficult for me to explain, but you too will feel a significant difference when you are married. The position of WIFE carries with it an increased respect for you as a woman and as a loving being and someone whose love moves outside of self.

Having a husband brings so much joy in so many areas. What absolutely amazes me is that you get "upgraded" benefits just by making such statements as "I have a reservation for Mr. and Mrs." or "Let me let you speak to my husband. I like for him to handle these matters." People, in general, make assumptions about your status and respond to you differently when they know you are married. When my husband and I started dating, I realized that I had to release some of the negotiation power to my then boyfriend/fiancé. Prior to releasing the negotiation task to him, I believed that I was the world's greatest negotiator in every area—daily purchases, car repairs, travel arrangements, and purchasing other goods and services. However, I soon found out that my husband had the ability to negotiate even harder; ask tough, targeted questions; and have discussions that are only fitting between men. I now proclaim that men are the best negotiators, but we ladies cannot know that if we do not rely on them. Just about anything you can do for yourself, a good man can add value to and perhaps do better. After all, isn't your life too busy to carry the entire load?

I was also glad to lie next to my husband one cold morning in Florida. While I am always happy to be next to him, I was truly appreciative of him as my husband that morning, knowing that I had his body heat to blanket me. How sexy was that? There was absolutely no sin involved. He was my husband and it was my right to receive all of his body heat. It is the moments like those that resonate within.

There are many perks for both men and women in the discussion of why should I get married. One of the critical reasons marriage is so important comes from its importance to the social, spiritual, and intellectual development of children. Research from the Department of Health and Human Services states that children raised in homes where a strong marriage and family life exist are more likely to succeed academically and attend college. They are also prone to be physically and emotionally healthier. Additionally, marriage benefits children by presenting a healthy view of relationships, which leads to fewer incidents of divorce among them as adults.

The research also indicates that children who grow up in a married, two-parent home receive natural training in conflict resolution and management. Further, children reared in homes of married parents are less likely to become sexually active early. Marriage certainly has its advantages; we must also remember that the family is the first introduction many of us experience as the meaning and purpose of community.

Thoughts to Ponder

What advantages do you see to being married?

What advantages do you see to being single?

Do you want to be married or single? Please explain.

Perhaps Marriage is Not For Me

Perhaps marriage is not for you. Marriage is not for everyone. Marriage requires a level of maturity that being single does not. Marriage is unique and has an entirely different level of ownership, accountability, and responsibility that being single does not. Also, if you have a pattern of giving away the cow and the milk in all of your relationships, there must come a time when you choose to close down the dairy and prepare yourself for marriage. Why continue to settle? There is no harm in preparing yourself for marriage.

Perhaps you are one of those women who can live without marriage. If so, do you ever wonder "what if?" Marriage can be miraculous, even when it brings rough seasons. Imagine having an earthly partner by your side forever—someone you unite with by choice. Being married does not mean that you find someone to complete you. It is naïve to believe that there is one man on this earth who can do that, specifically because each spouse should be complete when they enter into marriage. Yet, you can find someone to complement you. God has put together a beautiful blueprint of marriage based on mutual sacrifice. There is no other love like the love that comes from marriage. It is unlike the love you may have with your child, which contains feelings of obligation and the continuation of your legacy. Marriage is a choice. Can you imagine being married to someone who has decided to love you in this manner? Can you imagine choosing to love someone in that manner? The bond of marriage is quite miraculous because it is a decision, made by both parties, to love unselfishly and unconditionally, placing the other's feelings, heart, and spirit above their own.

While the media, family, and friends may degrade marriage, it is the last standing institution where commitment means something. Marriage gives us a safe place to be vulnerable and have a loving partner, particularly when you both have done your due diligence in seeking professional help, praying, and getting to know each other. Marriage restores the belief that with true love and a lot of hard work, people can stay committed to each other.

Marriage, just like everything else worth having in life, will have its ups and downs and will require a lot of hard work. After all, combining two imperfect individuals who have individual stories and bonding them together for life takes effort to sustain.

Every woman should have the opportunity to experience a good marriage. I do not believe you should get married for the sake of getting married, because everyone else is getting married, because you were asked. I believe women should prepare themselves for marriage and for sustaining that marriage if the opportunity presents itself because they love and respect themselves enough to enter into the most special and sacred of commitments.

Marriage teaches the power of teamwork. Marriage allows you to experience, as well as express, the apex of love. It is the Biblically defined way of procreation. It is a great place of friendship and the discovery of life together. It is a shared burden where you do not have to do everything yourself. I do realize that my desire for all women to have the opportunity to be married may be controversial. Some of my ideas about transitioning and preparing to be a wife may be controversial. That is absolutely fine. Marriage is a choice that you must make with a full scope of information. Marriage is more than a sheet of paper, more than a partnership; it is a holy and divinely spiritual relationship with God and an established covenant. For sexually active individuals, marriage upgrades you, not only in the world and within your family, but with God.

Thoughts to Ponder

Have you been married before? If so, why? If no, why not?

Why do you think God places such value on marriage?

Section Three

Analyzing Negative Behavior

Introduction

Single women certainly face several misconceptions, which sprawl like invasive graffiti on the walls of their lives. It is important to take some time to evaluate where all of this stuff comes from in an introspective manner. We must understand that multiple roads lead to the fountain of thoughts that pour from our minds and our hearts. In a quest to become wives, we must survey, identify, assess, reconsider, and become what we desire.

How Did I Get Here?

Take a moment to look at yourself and your surroundings. Go ahead… I can wait. Now ask yourself "How did I get here?" The truth is that we come to a particular place because of our thoughts. In other words, we are what we think and a result of what we have thought for a prolonged period of time. We have beliefs inside of us and these beliefs require energy that we release. Notice how individuals release their beliefs through their facial expressions, clothes, responses, hands, feet, friends, and so forth. Our beliefs can be overcome once we focus on the goal of removing negative beliefs. If you take time, make it a practice to identify these hindering beliefs and then work to get rid of them; they will soon have no other choice but to disappear. The progressive and positive beliefs that you have instilled will appear in their place.

You can look around and tell that most people do not have energy to change their beliefs. You see that they need to be changed—and perhaps they know they need to change—but there is no change taking place. When I go for months without exercising, I constantly tell myself it's too early in the morning to go to the gym, I would rather be in bed for one last minute with my husband, or I am not that overweight so gaining a few pounds will not hurt that much. If I do not recognize these beliefs are attempting to dwell within me, even though this is not who I am, I will soon become what I speak. Consequently, when a negative belief about going to the gym is trying to take over my mind, I make a conscious effort to focus my thoughts on my ultimate goal: working out and better overall health. To change this, first, I must look in the mirror and recognize that my clothes are fitting a bit more snugly. The energy I need to expend to change may begin with putting my exercise clothes next to my bed. The next day I may take another step and go to bed early, and the following day I may take another step and inform my husband that I have to get out of bed. Finally, I am back in the gym because I made an effort to control what I put in my head.

We can expend a lot of energy toward a belief that is not doing us any good. Your beliefs may be that you will not find Mr. Right or your soul mate or that he must have this or that before you look his way. You must de-energize these beliefs and develop new ones that invite what you desire. Say and believe that you will be happily married someday—that you believe that you will make a great wife. Tell yourself you believe that you should not be concerned about what he brings to the table but more concerned about what you bring to the table. Have an attitude, mindset, and outlook that say you are in preparation for a great man.

Thoughts to Ponder

Do you ever get lonely at night?

Do you ever have regrets about how you have handled relationships in the past?

Do you believe that you could have what it takes to be a wife, particularly if you made it a high priority?

Section Three

It's All About Me

Can you agree with this: that you have lived with and focused on YOU long enough? Focusing on YOU is not the key to marriage. One of the keys to marriage is knowing what you like and how you like it. In this case, you could remain single and remain in the paradigm-preserving mindset of being single and live happily-ever-after with and by yourself. However, the truth of the matter is that marriage requires you to understand what a man needs and likes.

Another key is knowing how to communicate with your man and meet his needs. This is vital to moving from a paradigm-preserving mindset to a paradigm-modifying mindset. Paradigm-preserving is only about SELF, while paradigm-modifying is about both SELF and OTHERS.

If you want to be a broker, entrepreneur, executive, Navy SEAL, Green Beret, or whatever you want to be in life, you have to figure out the process. You strategize and look at the blueprint of how to give the holder of what you need everything they require. To progress in Corporate America, we must figure out the qualifications, degrees, and experiences needed to obtain a particular position and/or status, and then we meet those needs. We do not require nor expect Corporate America to spoil us, be honest with us, or meet all of our requirements.

I am reminded of a friend who wanted a promotion in the human resources field. She looked into the requirements of several schools in order to gather and weigh the cost, options, and sacrifices. Even though my degree is not in human resources, she called me several times and sent multiple text messages seeking my guidance during her decision-making process. I wonder if she looked for a blueprint on relationships as methodically as she sought out the prerequisites of a degree.

A relationship is a partnership, and we need to be just as methodical about pursuing prerequisites and being successful in relationships as we are in areas that simply focus on us.

Our fears and insecurities make us stubborn about relinquishing a paradigm-preserving mindset. They are a detouring mechanism born out of the fear of being hurt, and they prevent us from reaching our heart's desires. To conquer them, we must relinquish being hard, tough, and challenging and embrace being soft, tender, and loving.

Thoughts to Ponder

Do you tend to focus only on self and those closest to you? If yes, do you believe you can modify your thought processes by considering the possibility of others feeling needed in your space?

When it comes to relationships, what are your fears?

Who are the individuals in your life who make you feel like number one?

How does being number one feel? Could you allow someone else to feel as though they are number one?

If You are Near a Mirror, Go Stand There

Look in the mirror and thoroughly observe "You, Inc." Look for your purpose, your motivations, your history, and your knowledge (or the lack thereof) as you study and meditate on self. Figure out what your mindset is regarding relationships. When you messed up, what happened? How did you respond? How hurt were you? Who guided you? When you succeeded in areas of your relationships, why did you succeed? Is your mind right for a relationship? List each relationship and itemize all the wrongs and the rights, as perceived by you. You want your mind to be in the right place so that it will be right in time for a relationship.

If we look back over our lives, we can see that both our deep and surface thoughts have guided our paths. These beliefs can be great or can act as shackles (also known as strongholds) that prevent us from reaching our dreams. Our unmanaged fears are at the root of our strongholds. In order to break free of these strongholds, we have to look beyond the surface and get to those fears—even the subconscious ones. If you tend to always put yourself in a positive light or simply have a hard time with self-examination, then survey a few of your friends, former relationship partners, and family members. This is going to be really tough, so only take it on if you really want to receive food for thought and are ready for it. To get honest feedback, provide them with a safety net, such as a signed oath that says you will not get angry with them and promise them a gift if you do not keep your word. The more personable, in-depth, and sincere the comments, the darker or more solemn you are likely to feel. Yet, remember this is ammunition in your quest to become better. Perhaps you are a person who easily voices your opinion about others, but since it is your day to just listen, you may feel very overwhelmed. It is okay. Keep in mind that you do not have to know what to do about the feedback right away, nor do you have to do anything with it immediately. This step is about getting this necessary observational information first. Once you have it in hand, set aside some time to absorb it, meditate on it, and allow change to come from what it reveals through prayer.

Thoughts to Ponder

Did your "mirror" reveal things that people and your conscious have consistently stated that you needed to change?

Were you honest with yourself?

Did you seek input from family members? If so, what was the feedback?

What would happen if you posted reminders around your home about the things the mirror revealed? Try it.

Section Three

Going Behind the Scenes

Single women, in general, do not seek out married women and ask them for their marriage blueprint. Perhaps you reject or disregard the advice of some married women because they do not have a college degree that garners your respect. However, many married women have "degrees" in life, marriage, and putting a man first that you lack. Society helps us view married women in such a downgraded way because everything is about status and self. People get caught up in being status-driven, believing it brings success. Women decide very early on in their career path to give their entire life over to that career, even if it means devoting sixty to ninety hours a week to it. The expectation is that success is assured. Nothing in society guides us in the direction of being successful as a wife. When we look around, there is not a great promotion of family or a simple blueprint that gives us the history of pre- and post-industrialization eras for women, showing us how to take the good from both time periods.

Sometime during the 20th century, women stopped focusing on making family a priority and began to focus instead on getting a college degree, starting a career, and then, somewhere down the road, considering marriage and starting a family. Society's emphasis on family has shifted and unless you have been raised in a strong, traditional family that emphasizes family and marriage values, it is extremely easy to live a very independent, isolated life where all you have to focus on is yourself. Because of this, for many women the first thoughts that come to mind when they think about a man are "What can he do for me?" "How can he help me get to where I am trying to go?" and "Is he trying to go where I am trying to go?" Today's woman receives very little direction in the area of paradigm shift. The focus is pro-education and pro-everything that leads to a better you; yet, education and all those other things do not make a woman a better wife. When a woman is at home with her husband, the way she interacts with him and the way they love each other boils down to basic human life principles: how they talk to one another, express themselves, treat each other, and work together. Our grandparents had the formula to stay together, even though today's woman is more educated, has acquired more, and has achieved more success. Despite it all, she is unable to have solid relationships over a long period of time.

Thoughts to Ponder

Describe your profile on the job?

Describe your profile with your children?

Describe your profile with your girlfriends?

Describe your profile with men?

Draw a table that allows you to compare your profiles across job, family, girlfriends, and men. What differences, if any, exist? Please explain if no differences or only a few differences exist?

Paradigm-Preserving Models of a Relationship – The Don'ts

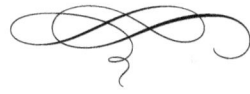

Let me expose you to three relationship-understanding models in hopes of liberating you from a self-preserving, paradigm-preserving mindset and shift you toward a paradigm-modifying mindset. These models are examples of the paradigm-preserving mindsets. Staying within one or more of these models means that it will be difficult, but not impossible, to get to your desired goal of being married. These relationship-understanding models are equity, investment, and upgrade.

Equity Model: The equity model is similar to a checklist. Equity represents the notion that everything in a love relationship is split fifty-fifty and a checklist of "items of responsibility" for both parties exists. This list is constantly evaluated to ensure that both parties are doing their share and one is not giving more than the other. This model is all about perceived equality. One of the many fallacies in the equity model is that only a perfect person who does not make mistakes and who is morally right can truly assign unbiased equality. All of us have a different value system, so most people will always assume that they are doing more than people recognize. It would be very difficult to tell someone they are not pulling their share without it leading to a very defensive confrontation with that person beginning to list several ways in which they contribute to the relationship followed by a list of things that the other is not giving to the relationship. Men, in particular, simply avoid this type of a "fair share" conversation and keep their thoughts internal. So, how can you truly evaluate equity? Defining equality in a relationship is difficult, even if an initial written, notarized agreement was in place!

In an equity relationship, both partners should give fifty-fifty within the relationship, or their best, which in most cases is a one hundred percent personal effort toward making the relationship successful. However, the reality is that you cannot measure someone's contribution to a relationship. What you perceive as thirty percent could actually be that individual's one hundred percent. I have come to learn that a relationship consists of two individuals who have had two different environments, two different sets of gifts, and two different areas of expertise, along with many other unique aspects about them. This makes your partner's way of communicating feelings completely different from yours. Further, their sacrifice or contribution to the relationship could be intangible, meaning you cannot taste, feel, or see it, even though it exists. Therefore, if you believe in the equity theory regarding relationships, you should not focus on the visible or tangible contributions; instead, you should simply focus on all of the contributions as well as the reality that you may give more and should be willing to give more.

Think about it—what person wants to reside in a home that has stipulations and contracts on mandatory contributions necessary to make the other person happy? Why not let the contributions be unspoken without a scorecard of who is contributing the most followed by an attempt at equilibrium? Give what you consider your one hundred percent and do it with love without expecting one hundred percent in return. Women who model relationships based on the equity theory tend to have discussions that center around what is "fair" versus structuring the relationship around a woman's natural design.

For example, should things become overwhelming and that person truly requires things of you that you cannot mentally and physically give, I suggest having a conversation that does not involve you saying, "I give more to the relationship." Instead, I suggest a conversation conveying that you feel overwhelmed but still desire to please him and need his help in certain areas to better position you to focus on what he needs or desires in the relationship. As a matter of fact, let him decide what his areas of excellence are or where his talents thrive best.

There are other major flaws with this equity theory mindset. First, participants use a one-dimensional measure of fairness or equity. You cannot measure someone's input like you do your weight or height. A relationship is not like baking a cake, where two cups of flour, one teaspoon of baking powder, and two teaspoons of vanilla extract create a perfect cake with the right smell, taste, rise, and moisture.

Second, in a relationship based on the equity theory, you only focus on the outcome, and the ultimate value of a relationship is beyond perceived outcome or reward. Thus, in this process the focus is never on enjoying more important and in-depth connections that lead up to the reward.

Third, the idea of fairness is hard to understand. Yet, equity theory relationships are built around the concept of fairness, which carries a lot of weight and focus in the relationship to the extent of governing our behavior. The motivation for doing something for the benefit of the relationship is based primarily on one's perceived fairness, contributions, rewards, and punishments.

Hopefully, you do not prescribe to a paradigm-preserving relationship model where both partners decide the relationship should be governed by some form of equality. How do you determine who will keep track of the equality? Do you stipulate that every meal will be split fifty-fifty? Such a tracking system makes it hard to function in a loving relationship. It becomes mentally taxing, which affects the longevity of a relationship. I understand that no one wants to feel used or taken for granted and that this self-preserving mode of equality may be an attempt to keep you from being used and abused. However, equality will never work for the woman who embraces wanting a true man. You will never want a man who offers to take you to dinner Dutch-style.

No woman or man wants to be constantly measured and evaluated in a relationship. You want your man to represent who he is supposed to be. One of the loopholes of the equity principle is that it does not work across the spectrum of relationship situations. How would you feel if you were asking to contribute your half each time you engage in an activity?

Could it be that you pursue equality in your relationships because of what has happened in the past in a previous relationship? Perhaps you have watched other women, in your opinion, "be taken advantage of," "not be a strong woman," or "be used." Consequently, you attempt to ensure that similar occurrences do not happen to you. Yet, the truth of the matter is, there will be times in a relationship where you will find yourself carrying the load and giving more than your mate, which is more likely to be the case for women. Equality takes out the element of what you truly want in a relationship.

Investment Model: This model is similar to risk management. A woman operating in this model goes into a relationship with the mindset that she is investing her time, her resources, and other resources with a desired goal in mind. Whenever she gets the inkling that the outcome is not going to yield the results she anticipated while choosing to invest, everything changes. A woman who thinks within the investment model is typically calculating and conservative. This individual does not typically go into a relationship headfirst because she is trying to reduce risk. She is always going to be at a high evaluation level, always wanting to know where she stands, what the return is, if she is investing too much, or if she is giving too much.

Unlike the equity model, the investment model has its advantages from the perspective of planting and sowing seeds with an anticipated goal. If the investment model is to work, then you must invest with the intention of doing well for the relationship and not only for self. There is no such thing as a risk-free investment; hence, there is no such thing as a risk-free relationship. Every relationship is a risk. Every investment, whether it is conservative, calculated, or a sure thing, is a risk. Every investment does not yield a high return. The bottom line is that you have to leave some latitude in reality. Any investment firm will show you their data that predicts returns, but they have no way of guaranteeing the outcome because anything can happen.

You must have the same mindset and principle you have toward an investment portfolio when it comes to a relationship. Go into a relationship with data, research, and historical events, and diversify your strategy and approach to the relationship with the understanding that there are no guarantees. You may also sow in one place but reap in another place. Let me illustrate. Let's say you meet a man you believe to be Mr. Right and you want to do everything for him, including cooking. You purchase cookbooks and complete several cooking lessons all with the intention that your skills will forever be used to satisfy the one you think is Mr. Right. All of a sudden, you are no longer with Mr. Right. While he ended up being the temporary benefactor of your investment, you still have to eat, and the true Mr. Right headed your way will want to eat too. Thus, you will still get a high return on your investment.

Do not allow yourself to be narrowly focused when it comes to your investments in yourself or anyone else. For every improvement you make within yourself, for every skill you develop, you will eventually reap the rewards of your investment. Why believe your efforts are in vain? It is not about what happens to us more than it is about how we respond to what happens to us and how we improve ourselves, even if the goal of being with someone was not met.

I do have to acknowledge that everything we do in an effort to get into or maintain a relationship is not great. I also believe that, just like in every other life area, we have to learn from our mistakes. Some things we do, such as learning to speak softly, learning to be submissive, learning to have patience, or learning to cook, are all beneficial and add value to our lives—period. Thus, an investment in developing yourself always pays off! If necessary, do not be afraid to sever the ties and start over.

One of the fallacies of the investment model is that it can be difficult to determine what is done out of love and what is done out of expecting something in return. If you keep looking at a relationship based upon an investment, the only reason you will continue to put "money" into the "stock" is because of the return. If you do not see a return (e.g., an increase), chances are that other investments start to look better. So, if your stock is not performing in the manner that you believe is necessary to yield the proper return, then your natural instinct is to look at other stocks to see how they are performing. In your relationship, perhaps you just looked in the mirror and told yourself that you deserve better. With this mindset in place, you then find yourself surrounded by girlfriends and relatives who tell you, "Girl, you deserve better" or "I went to this social last night and there were doctors, lawyers, and billionaires at every turn. That's the kind of man you need to meet."

Perhaps you find yourself listening to a woman who is elated about the ways her husband treats her. You begin to compare your stock to other stock options, which leads to the thought that the grass is greener on the other side. But is the grass truly greener on the other side? With the investment mindset, could you ever marry anyone, as the grass could always be greener elsewhere? You do not consider that the grass may be painted for show, that it may be Astroturf (not real, but fabricated for a purpose), or that it might be heavily fertilized (meaning this couple goes beyond average to make their marriage work.)

If you approach life believing that you always have to get the best return on your investment in relationships, you will remain single. You will always be confronted with other options and possibilities, looking for better. Instead, you should become comfortable with understanding and loving your ten percent return, particularly if your ten percent makes you happy, even knowing there is a chance that another investment may get you twenty percent. This is the risk you take in a relationship. Just remember that the stock market eventually crashes in every cycle. At some point, you have to make a decision about who you want to be with and make a choice to feel great about your return.

Think about it. If you are in a relationship with a man who sees you as an investment, how can you determine if his acts of kindness are because he really loves you or because he sees you as a return on his investment? The only reason this man may be with you is because of what he thinks he can get in return, which may or may not be associated with like, lust, or love. No one wants to feel this way—being in a relationship because of a resulting career advancement, who they know, what they have, or what they can provide, and not because of love. The investment model eliminates the "just because" statements: "just because I love you," "just because I was thinking about you," and the like. The investment model prohibits or eliminates the natural evolution of intimacy in and of relationships. Intimacy naturally flows as you get closer to people and grow. While love should not blind us into bad judgment and decision-making, to structure your relationship purely within the investment model may take the natural intimacy out of it.

Upgrade Model: This model is similar to the investment model; however, it is focused on Upgrade! Upgrade! Upgrade! This is not the type of upgrade a wife receives by joining in matrimony with the one designed to love her. This is an upgrade that is all about self. This upgrade says a man's presence in her life is all about upgrading what and who she is and her status. This upgrade is based on status as the cake, the frosting, and the silver platter with a man as the cherry on top. The true litmus test of this relationship dynamic is if a woman's net worth increases as a result of being in the relationship.

This model raises many questions for you to answer. What am I getting out of a relationship with this man? How does this relationship make me better? What has been upgraded in my life by virtue of being in this relationship? How is my life better by being with this man? How has this man upgraded me? What networks have I been exposed to because of my relationship with this man? Under this model, if you were able to have a Mercedes-Benz before the relationship, then you would expect to be in a position to drive a Bentley because of the relationship. This idea underscores the true concept of the upgrade model. Women in this area are not focused on upgrades in premium areas of morality, better attitude, and such intrinsic characteristics. What if you enter into a relationship where you have to take care of a man or you find yourself taking care of a man at some point within the relationship? Let's face it, not many of us have parents, family, and friends who want us to do that. Accordingly, you will find yourself in re-evaluation mode, analyzing your situation and asking yourself, "What benefits am I getting out of this relationship? What is in it for me? All I can see is what I am putting into the relationship."

Perhaps you are getting smothered in love by someone who loves you unconditionally, who wants to marry you, and who respects you. The point here is that you should never view a relationship from the perspective of an upgrade. Eventually, your relationship will go through seasons where you will feel like you have little to boast about. Your love and evaluation of the relationship should not rest on the upgrade factor, especially when a two-second snap could put any of us in the position of being unemployed.

The fallacy of the upgrade model is that it does not give room for fluctuation in both good and bad markets. A recession in your relationship cannot be viewed as a sign to use an exit strategy. If your model is benefits driven, then you do not give yourself flexibility to deal with the fluctuation of uncontrollable circumstances. You may even feel that the outcome does not warrant your perpetual actions, so you stop giving toward the relationship. You tend to shut down if you are not given a particular benefit (e.g., attention, luxuries), which will drive a huge wedge in the relationship.

This model does not embrace the vows "for better or worse, for richer or for poorer," so it does not adequately prepare you for marriage and the seasons that may occur where your relationship or marriage may take a downturn. Pulling back and re-shifting because the cost outweighs the benefits does not typically resolve anything in a relationship, but instead drives partners further apart.

Knowing where you are in your thinking will assist in moving you forward.

If your relationship fits even slightly or somewhat within one of these models, you are definitely in a paradigm-preserving mindset. Perhaps you believe that the relationship should be equally beneficial to both parties. Once the cost of being in the relationship outweighs the benefits, you are likely to jump ship.

Another way of treating a relationship is as if it is partitioned into what belongs to you and what belongs to your partner. You will constantly work toward a goal of what you perceive to be fair. You then create and constantly modify the rules of your relationship to reach a level of fairness where you attempt to maintain equal treatment. If fairness does not exist in a specific situation, then additional modifications must be made to accomplish equity.

Maybe you treat your relationship like an investment—what you put into your relationship is directly related to what you get out of the relationship. You are making constant comparisons of other investments within the relationship and outside of the relationship. In many situations, you compare choices within the context of gains and losses. The more you invest, (and the less other options appear to be rewarding or profitable), the more you are committed to the relationship, independent of your love for the other. To move into wifely swag, please shift from these models and do not allow them to govern your heart and mind during your transition process.

Thoughts to Ponder

Do you know your relationship model?

What paradigm-preserving model best describes how you govern your relationships?

What are the pros and cons of your relationship model?

Section Three

Listen to Your Internal / Hidden Layer

Women go through silent, internal struggles. We have moments where we really do not feel we are sufficient or as if there is something intrinsically wrong with us. Now, do not bail out on me with thoughts of "I know who I am, I know my self-worth, Mrs. Author Lady!" Allow me to challenge you with a thought meant to simmer: it is easier for you to dismiss this thought claiming self-awareness or self-empowerment rather than admit that there could be something in you that a particular man has challenged. Whether we want to admit it or not, I believe we all have insecurities and shortcomings. We may not verbalize them, but they become obvious and intertwine with how we deal with men. Country music singer Colin Raye has a song, "We're Really Not That Different," that drive this point home.

The deeper issue is that often these internal struggles suggest that you are inadequate, incomplete, or insufficient in some way. Pause here to listen to yourself. Close the book and have a moment of self-truth. We are made to always have a degree of vulnerability and a degree of imperfection. This is why we value trust, fidelity, loyalty, and similar things so much. Looking at these areas of belief in others (and in self) exposes our internal struggles, hurts, and fears. That is why infidelity or an unwanted breakup leads to questions, such as "What didn't I do?" or "What didn't I give him?" and statements, such as "It's his loss, not mine" and "I deserve better, and better is right around the corner." Why would a very secure, highly self-esteemed person ever consider these thoughts if this quiet internal struggle did not really exist? The internal struggle could be just simply admitting your fears. Perhaps you think you cannot fly to the altitude of holistic success you have set for yourself and nothing is ever enough. Could your laundry list of things you want in a man be a camouflage for the insecurities you feel and your list just pampers those insecurities? Does that list stop you from exposing, facing, and overcoming your inner blockades? What are some of the things that could have gotten you here? Some very independent, self-assured women may have already skipped this section, unable to think of a time that a man was better without the well-accomplished, self-esteem-laden woman they are in their lives. However, if you are still reading, let us look into the paradigm-preserving mindset a little further.

Thoughts to Ponder

Have you ever unjustifiably distrusted a man?

What are your insecurities?

What are your shortcomings?

Have you discussed your insecurities and shortcomings with anyone? If not, why not? If so, what was the result?

Paradigm-Preserving Mindset— A Deeper Look

I have mentioned the paradigm-preserving mindset on several occasions in this body of work. Let's take a more in-depth look at how we get into paradigm-preserving mindsets. We know that a paradigm-preserving mindset is not innate to all women because the paradigm-preserving mindset is not found in all women. The paradigm-preserving mindset begins in the foundational and formative years of women's lives when they are told over and over again to "Be a strong woman," "Get your own stuff," "Be independent," "Don't rely on a man to take care of you," "Get your degree," "You can do bad all by yourself," and so forth. Not only have today's women heard these messages, but they have seen them while being raised in female-led, strong, single-parent households. Corporate America has further taught women to be "slaves to the system" to achieve success that has a ceiling but not to value family as part of successful achievement. Chances are that most women today had a childhood image of a single woman as the pillar of success. Mom is probably a hero.

Then again, during the most formative years of their lives, maybe these women were taught to "get your own; do not depend on a man…" This is anti-marriage language. For those women raised by both parents, there is a high probability that they either witnessed a divorce or watched their mothers being suppressed. Mom's life may not have been suppressed at all (at least not by her standards) but instead a conscious decision to dedicate one hundred percent to her family and marriage and to bettering herself. In either case, the decision was made that the road their mom took is not the road these women want to take. They never consider the possibility that perhaps, like me, mom and dad had no blueprints on relationships and marriage. They also do not consider that the dynamics of someone else's marriage are too difficult to comprehend, analyze, and solve. Perhaps, a more productive approach is looking for positive nuggets of wisdom from whatever relationship scenario existed in an effort to build a healthy model to emulate.

As women grow older and mature, they surround themselves with like-minded women who have similar views about the roles women have in relationships. These like-minded women are also in a paradigm-preserving mindset. Therefore, they reinforce all that was previously heard and seen growing up, such as "Girl, get your own stuff," "Work hard, get your own car, get your own crib, and don't let a man do that for you," and "If you do get a man, he needs to be straight by having this and that." Chances are that most of these women who are pretty avid about what is needed regarding men and relationships have never had a man or perhaps failed at relationships. They are deeply entrenched in this paradigm-preserving mode and will perhaps die there. Many women have identified these self-defeating thought patterns and can even point to how they have affected their progress. Sheila is one of many women who shared her story with me during the development of this book and is a prime example.

Sheila is a successful entrepreneur in her thirties. While she could have married in her twenties, Sheila admits that she could not have stayed married because she thought she knew everything. She bought into the belief that she was the prize in any relationship, so regardless of whom she dated, her behavior signaled that she was the prize and they were beneath her. Sheila thought that the formula she used in her successful business would also work in her relationships, causing her to treat all men like those who worked for her. Sheila admits that she was not only mean to men, but she was also mean to herself because she ignored the signs of bad relationships. She feared it would appear she could not "manage" her relationships properly.

Another aspect of life that nurtures paradigm-preserving mindsets is personal success. Say you do exactly what you have been told to do and get to a point where you do not have to depend on a man. You have been successful in this paradigm-preserving mindset. You have a degree, money in the bank, you own a home, and drive the car of your dreams. You obtained all of these things within your paradigm-preserving mindset; however, none of this stuff challenges the paradigm-preserving system. Now, ask yourself if you are totally and completely happy. When I ran this question through my head periodically, the answer was NO, yet I would not move in a direction that would get me to the happiness I desired. It was easier to continue operating in a fashion that I was most comfortable, where I had more confidence and control. Chances are, when you ask yourself the same question, your answer is also NO, unless you have been ordained to live a life of celibacy and be by yourself. Otherwise, there is still this desire inside of you to be with a man and have a family.

For me, the two pending questions became can I have both and how can I obtain them. I was nowhere close to the answers to these questions because I had unconsciously surrounded myself with similar paradigm-preserving women. Like me, your transition begins when you ask yourself how to embrace the paradigm-shifting mindset that gives you the attitude, latitude, and freedom to have a career and be a wife without losing self. This paradigm-shifting mindset begins when you stop focusing solely on you and allowing your past negative relationship experiences to further solidify why you should remain in the paradigm-preserving mode. In other words, do not have a mindset of survival of the fittest or not putting your heart and soul into a relationship.

Thoughts to Ponder

What are your views about marriage?

What are your views about married women?

Did anyone ever teach you or coach you on how to be a wife?

Paradigm-Shifting to Paradigm-Modifying

If you are reading this page, you are in a great place. You are considering the possibility that you may be in need of a paradigm shift in your mindset, ultimately affecting your thoughts and behavior. If you do not desire to have a wonderful husband, then you have chosen to go through life being single, lacking that special man who connects with you and gives you a safe place to rest. While I desired a husband, I was unconsciously doing everything that attracted Mr. Wrong. Even though I could determine he was not right for me, I lacked a plan to attract Mr. Right. Based on all of the accounts and information implanted in my head, I believed all I had to do was cast my net and find a man who would be honored to be my husband if I was only willing to overlook a lot of his flaws. In hindsight, I am now convinced that God had this man's best interest in mind. After all, what man in his right mind would want a self-centered, headstrong, non-submissive, "all that," bossy, mouthy woman who truly believed she was the biggest asset in the relationship?

What I needed was a paradigm shift. The day I realized I needed to transition from my old paradigm to a new paradigm was when life began to truly blossom into a red rose more beautiful than anything I could imagine. I recall one morning watching a relative make breakfast for everyone and wondering if she found marriage easy. As I was analyzing her, I heard her boldly state, "Antoinette is a beautiful, attractive lady…" No surprise there; I had heard those words before. As I was about to smile and say thank you, she finished her statement by saying, "As soon as the right man comes into her life, there is no telling what she can do." I asked myself if I heard this woman correctly. Did she just say what I think she said? Did she just tell me and everyone who was listening that a man could make me better? Luckily, before hearing this statement, I was in some way prepared to have an open mind and simply listen without a response. Her statement was all I needed to finally get the picture that I needed to focus on meeting Mr. Right. Focusing on meeting Mr. Right was not necessarily about attracting a man, but about transitioning and preparing so I would be in a better position to know and present the characteristics of a wife if the opportunity presented itself. I also believed that prayer and my synergy of thoughts would draw Mr. Right toward me. In other words, I had to believe and act like Mr. Right would enter my life.

Before the realization of my shift, I was bold in my statements to several men who tried their best to get into my inner circle. Even when I met my husband, I was still going through this transition. Luckily, God sent the right man to me because, while I was in transition and my thought processes and behavior still manifested under the old paradigm, my now-husband set the record straight with me several times. Consistently, when my old self appeared, he did not hesitate to tell me that my behavior was unacceptable. I remember telling him while we were dating and also while we were engaged, "Please understand that I do not know all there is about being a wonderful wife. Please have patience with me and help me transform into the person I want to be." I was telling him to hold steady and strong with me as I transitioned and that if he did just that, we both would be the beneficiaries of my growth. Even if he did not have the endurance to hang tight with me, I knew for sure that I would benefit from my growth. I also had a friend or two who I would call whenever the "Antoinette with the big ego" showed up, the one who would retract to bad habits and proclaim, "I don't need this. I am better than this. There are other men who would love to be in his shoes!" I was smart enough to tell my friends, "Although I am complaining, do not let me trip myself up. He is a great man and it would hurt to lose him, so do not let me get in my way." They heard my cry and gave feedback that aligned with my wishes. Everyone aligned with my wishes as I spoke my desires into reality. My now-husband as well as all my friends knew I had a desire to be a wife. They knew it through the way that I was always focusing on my transition.

As I continued to make my shift from the old paradigm to the new paradigm, the anti-wifely words of so many women became more salient, leaving me to realize that I once sounded just like them and thought like them. How I yearned for these women to understand how they were trapped in a paradigm that could only lead to unhappiness and a constant cycle of bad relationships. This cycle would not only affect them but also those who were watching them, including their children and other women. Let us transition into a nation of women who are bold enough to consider that our way of thinking can potentially destroy who we are along with who our family and friends are designed to be.

Shifting to a new paradigm means shifting to a better life; it also means shifting to a better relationship and to a better you. This is a change that will impact current and future generations. After all, if you can undertake a shift in your behavior, attitude, and outlook for your business and your job, why not undertake one for your relationship? While many things can be easy for a woman, balancing a husband, children, and a career requires strategic planning, good choices, mental preparation, new skills and knowledge, mentors and role models, and practice. Initiating a new relationship paradigm will require hard work. There is nothing easy about it. However, the sooner you begin, the sooner you will reap the rewards.

Being married requires teamwork, which can feel like a daunting task for most independent women, particularly if it is not necessary for career advancement and requires self-sacrifice. You cannot be divergent and fuzzy in your process. Your transition requires an intentional and diligent effort to pluck you from your comfort zone. A good marriage and a good husband do not just happen because you want them to happen. Stop asking men to take you as you are. This translates as your having no desire to grow and says his opinion and desired changes in you do not matter. Would you marry someone who said this to you?

Think about this scenario: A successful and ambitious woman who has achieved academic and career success meets the diamond in the rough, a man who is just as educated as she is. In other words, what they both bring to the table is an even wash. However, the longevity of the relationship depends on the core of each of them. They both put their degrees on the wall. Everything is equal. Now they have to see how connected they can be as human beings and hopefully not just exist and relate through the exterior, material stuff.

Your relationship will either weather the storm or drown in it, given your human connection or lack thereof. Relationships do not survive because of all the plaques on the wall and other accolades on the table; they thrive on the very core of your character and your mindset. Just like you bring more to the table than your accolades, so does he.

Thoughts to Ponder

What do you bring to the relationship table? Please prioritize and explain.

Has anyone ever told you that you would make a great wife? If so, why? If no, why do you think they haven't?

Section Three

Section Four

Putting the Transition into Motion

Introduction

When we operate in the paradigm-preserving mode, we preserve the very thought patterns that guide our actions away from what we truly desire. When we are in this mode, it is difficult for us to think outside the box or change what we know and start with a clean slate. A paradigm-modifying thought, on the other hand, helps us view life through a different lens—one outside our comfort zone. We begin to consider things that were otherwise unimaginable. However, when we take applicable and practical steps to shift our thought patterns, behaviors, and life practices, we can move in a determined manner toward our goal of becoming wives. These next few pages are some of the practical tools that you can apply toward becoming a wife-in-preparation.

So How Do I Shift?

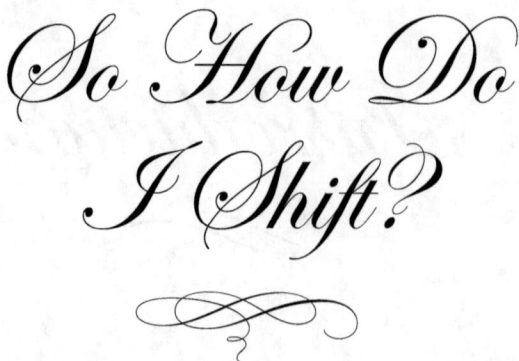

You've seen the movies where the psychologist asks his or her clients to relax, lay back on the couch, and reflect on their childhood or a particular event. Placing yourself in a relaxing position while someone guides your thoughts allows you to explore, uncover, and expand those thoughts. During paradigm modification, you begin to think in revolutionary ways that differ from your old, paradigm-preserving thought processes, which allows you to see problems entirely differently. As long as you remain within the paradigm-preserving thought process, you continue to have the tendency to view the problem within a limited scope of imagination and may not see the "real problem." However, with a paradigm-modifying view, you can make an effort to broaden your understanding and expand beyond your current mindset. In this place, you are more likely to identify and focus on the real problem, ultimately leading to a better solution or understanding than you would have gained under the paradigm-preserving thoughts. Thinking outside the box forces you to find a better solution or get to a better understanding. Through paradigm-modifying practices, the "paradigm shift" begins to take place.

Have you ever observed the metamorphosis process of a butterfly? The butterfly starts off as an egg and learns to live as a caterpillar. By all accounts, the caterpillar seems happy and content but operates with limited capacity and travels at a very slow speed. Before the caterpillar transforms into a beautiful butterfly that can fly, land, sample many flowers, and perhaps take part in a wedding, it must first go through a very unattractive chrysalis stage. In the chrysalis stage, the caterpillar is covered in a protective coating for a certain period while the transformation process continues. You will go through a similar metamorphosis while transforming from who you are now to someone who is able to deliver the best of yourself. When you get your mind right, the right behavior follows along with a new philosophy, structure, and priorities.

As you are making this transition, you may feel like I felt—that the paradigm shift at times feels like the wilderness. During my wilderness times, I constantly prayed for God to make me wife-like. After all, I was in a paradigm-preserving mode that taught me to think in an individualistic, strong-minded, vocal, and fiercely independent way. The only exception was my family. While I made exceptions and modifications in my prior relationships, I never fully committed to transforming myself into a wife according to God's standards. I had nothing to lose and everything to gain. One of the primary differences between you and me is that, with this book, you have the roadmap to change.

As in any wilderness, you will be unsure of what lies ahead; however, you know that if you keep pressing forward, you will eventually come out of it. So, while you are in the wilderness, what does not make sense initially will make sense later, and what seems irrelevant in the beginning will become relevant later. Do not seek rewards, although they are likely to come. As a matter of fact, you will discover more of your ability to transition to a better place and thus a better outcome.

Thoughts to Ponder

What are some old perspectives about relationships that you could trash?

What are some new perspectives about relationships that you could gain?

What steps have you taken to gain them?

The Spring Cleaning Approach

For my fellow independent ladies who are ready to clear out old paradigms, or for those who want a methodological approach to becoming a wife, I submit to you a deconstruction process that is similar to spring cleaning. When you spring clean your home, you do a thorough cleaning of the entire house, donating and trashing things you once considered valuable and necessary. Spring cleaning tends to occur when the weather turns nice, the air is fresh, and the flowers are blooming. Once you go through the paradigm spring-cleaning process, you will look like a garden full of blossoming flowers—some fully opened and ready to pull in all the rain and sunshine and some still buds. Everyone will know you are in transition; you will not have to say a word since your glow and growth will speak for itself.

Before we go into the spring-cleaning process, let's take a look at Maria. Maria is approximately forty-five years old, Hispanic, and twice married. Her first marriage ended in divorce and her second marriage ended in death. When I interviewed Maria, she was quite surprised that family and friends judged her to be a good wife. Maria stated that she was taught her entire life how to be a good wife and how to cater to a man, so this was not her area of concern. When her husband died, Maria realized that she focused so much on being a wife that she forgot to focus on herself. At forty-five years old, for the first time in her life, Maria is starting the spring-cleaning process of discovering who she is and discarding the remnants from her marriages and her pre-marriage knowledge. She does not want to focus on another man until she focuses on herself. So, while Maria was good marriage material by everyone else's account, both she and her spouses knew otherwise.

It is difficult to make someone happy when you do not understand what makes you happy. Spring cleaning is a very tedious task for someone else to take on for you. Although the spring-cleaning process can never come too late, it is critical to engage in before you get married. We can easily identify those women who have been married and divorced. They either live with resentment or a state of exciting revelation where they have reflected, discovered, resolved, and moved forward.

Prevent yourself from living under the guidelines of your mother's way, your friend's way, or your family's way, which can ultimately lead to your "unhappy way." Do not let your life be a composite of what others have required of you. Know yourself and make your own requirements through the vision of wisdom. Wisdom is a combination of having the freedom to explore, learning from mistakes, periodically going through a self-reflection stage, listening to others, seeking knowledge and advice, being open to criticism, making good decisions, being able to decipher good and bad advice, monitoring individuals in your inner circle, being open to other views, and acknowledging that your wisdom is bound within your experience. Gaining wisdom is an ongoing process that you should engage in consistently.

Do not allow yourself to go through a nuclear episode—something as catastrophic and emotionally intense as a career collapse, loss of a loved one, or a divorce—before you engage in spring cleaning. If you are single, now is a great time to spring clean. When you are single, you have control over your entire timetable. Additionally, you can go through the spring-cleaning process by focusing solely on your own emotions and not the emotions of your partner.

If you are already in a relationship, then you have more of a challenge than ladies who are not. You will have to engage in spring cleaning while maintaining your current relationship. The man you are in a relationship with may not be comfortable enough to give you the latitude to take time for yourself and go through multiple changes before you look like a beautiful garden. When you are in a relationship, it can be difficult to communicate your spring-cleaning process without making the other person feel insecure or believing that it is the end. Some people do not know how to support you through a transformation process. While it will be difficult, it is possible. You will have to be transparent, communicate consistently to the person, and obtain the aid of professional services when necessary.

Regardless of your relationship status, getting professional help can create one of the safest, most structured environments for transformation. When you seek professional services, particularly those of someone who specializes in family and marriage counseling, you get a trained professional who can give you his or her unbiased judgment.

Spring cleaning is analogous to self-discovery. If done methodically, you should receive the same benefits you get from cleaning a window. We clean a window so that we may see clearly through the dust and dirt that has accumulated over time. Although the window still serves it purpose when dirty, it is not as clear as it could be. When it comes to "You, Inc.," perhaps your vision has been impaired. Aside from cleaning during spring cleaning, you also put things away or give away some items. Similarly, in our lives there are some things that we need to pack and things we need to give away, but if you do not take the time to spring clean, the junk will stay in your mind and be exposed.

Now let's get started with the spring-cleaning process. Although described in steps, this process may take months to complete.

Step 1: Purchase the prettiest notepad and write this title on it: "[Your Name] – I Am More Than What Meets the Eye – My Spring Cleaning Journey [Today's Date]." This notepad will become one of your most treasured items as well as your testimony to the steps you took to transition your life. Keep it for your eyes only and for at least two to three years subsequent to your growth.

Step 2: Brainstorm about everything you have been taught about relationships. When you brainstorm, think about both your current and past relationships and what you have learned from them all. Look for consistent, reiterated messages from yourself and others, consistent environmental factors, consistent/common themes in the character of men you have been involved with, and common beginnings and endings. Leave several blank pages in each of these areas, since additional concepts of what you have been taught about relationships will surface at different moments.

Step 3: Brainstorm about everything you desire in a relationship being sure to leave additional space to include additional desires. Attempt to ignore information obtained from society, media, family, and friends. Use your wildest imagination to attempt to tap into your innermost desires. My list included the following: forgiveness, growth, understanding, communication, love, friendship, trust, attraction, understanding, acceptance, security, God, and laughter.

Step 4: Use the brainstorming list you generated in the previous step to help you describe where you currently are. Be very honest with yourself, even with the things that may hurt when you write them.

Step 5: Write a list of lies that people have stated about you on one page. On the next page, write a list of truths that people have stated about you. Do not compile these lists with your eyes shut. If you find that a truth hurts, simply put your name next to the truth, and make a commitment to take control and change. For the items you listed under lies, try to understand why these lies have been told about you. Ask what you can do to reverse these lies, such as asking for clarification from others, seeking forgiveness, or accepting them for what they are.

Step 6: Describe the woman who you would like to be in a relationship. After you have generated this list, explore what is stopping you from being this type of woman. Ask yourself if you have cleaned your window to the best of your ability. If not, simply revisit your list. Some things may still look blurry to you, given that you do not have all the solutions at this very moment, but you have begun the cleaning process and that is a big deal.

Step 7: Stay within your notepad on one sheet of paper and draw a box. On a separate sheet of paper, draw a trash can. As you revisit all the previous steps, continue to deconstruct yourself by placing items about yourself that you would like to store away in writing on the box page. Items you would like to either trash or give away should be recorded on the trash page. I recall wanting to box away my level of independence. In other words, my high level of independence needed to stay boxed until I understood how to keep it in check and had the wisdom to know when to use it.

Step 8: Take what you have discovered about yourself and use it to maximize your potential. You now know more about yourself through deconstruction, honesty, and reflection, placing you in a better position to focus the mind on maximizing your potential to exhibit wife-like behaviors! Go get it! Reach high!

Your Friends and Yes, Your Mother

"Show me a controlling mother or family member, and I'll show you a single woman." How your mother conducts herself in her current and past relationships is an indicator of whether she can lead you on the road to becoming a great wife. Just like you do not want to marry a "mama's boy," no one wants to marry a mother's girl. You cannot free yourself of your mother, but you can decide what to share with her and when to seek her advice.

Here is guidance on how to structure your inner circle of family and friends. Teamwork makes the dream work, so size up the people who are occupying your space.

Get with Other Women Who Think the Way You Are Trying to Think. This area is so critically important. If we are missing something, we can often find it in a communal aspect. The knowledge that you cannot make all of this happen by yourself is part of maximizing your potential. No matter how highly independent you are or how many books you read, you are going to have to connect with other seasoned, strong women who are trying to think like you and who are trying to go where you are trying to go in order to make this happen. It goes back to the "village" concept where we say it takes a village to raise a child. What does it take to give birth to a truly authentic woman? It takes a village as well. The wrong women can talk you out of your destiny, while the right women can push you into it.

Seek a Diverse Group of Friends. I always believed it was a bad idea to only hang out with those who think like you and who are similar to you. I do believe this idiom to benefit you in the areas of religion, great work ethic, and positive attitude. However, I believe that, as a woman, you should have a mixture of resources in friends that you must consistently evaluate on what I call a "positive energy scale of 1 to 10." Only reach out to those resources that are a minimum of 8 on the scale. I personally prefer to deal with all positive individuals and quickly remove negative ones from my speed dial.

Take Inventory of Your Friends. You must survey people in your space. You cannot afford to have anti-marriage people within your inner circle. Instead, have positive individuals on your team to help and support you as you travel through this journey that is likely to open many doors for you and transform you into a better person. Always remember that you must prevent yourself from becoming a victim of anti-marriage visions and that you have the right to claim victory in your life when it comes to marriage.

Study Courtship Material and Married Individuals. Look beyond the surface when you examine the behaviors of the married couples you know. Examine the infrastructure of their marriage, the walls of their heart, and their decision-making closely. Pay attention to the ingredients that make the marriage productive. Do not be impressed by what looks good on the outside because that may not tell you what is on the inside. Look beyond the material things and more into the seeds that are sown in the relationship.

Position Your Team Members Appropriately. You must not only have the right people on your team, but they must be in the right position, especially given that what lies ahead is too valuable to trust to just your own mindset. Having the wrong person in the wrong position can take you to the wrong place. You must have people in your camp who will help you work diligently and who are skilled in their position and know when, where, what, and how to lead you.

Here is a suggested inventory of friends to keep in your inner circle.

- *Spiritual friends.* I consider these as friends who listen to your frustration but always lead you to the word of God and remind you to pray on the issue. These are the friends who never rush you into a decision and find quick solutions. These individuals will give you sound advice even if it is not what they practice.

- *Hangout friend.* This is the friend you call to just hang out at your home, next to the pool, or at the bar and with whom you simply talk about whatever comes to mind. This person just allows you to let your hair down and forget about all the stress. He or she does not have visible self-esteem issues and understands looking good, loving self, and respecting others. This person can keep secrets and may be the person you release your vulnerabilities to so that you can begin to analyze the sensitive areas of your life in order to begin moving forward.

- *Mentor/Career friends* (preferably with a family/husband as well). I think you should have several friends who have achieved more in their career than you have, both within and outside of your career path. These friends may not know anything about your personal life, but they can keep your career path grounded.

- *Mother or mother-like figure.* This is the person who just listens and may never have an opinion one way or the other. She may not be career-focused but knows how to raise a family, cook, and be a wife.

- *Sexy friend.* This person helps you rejuvenate the sexiness within you because you do want to be appealing. You can call and run an idea by her or ask for tips with honest feedback on your appearance. You can also share your thoughts and tips with her. You and your sexy friend may even trade off your most expensive dresses at times.

A suggested inventory of friends to remove from your inner circle:

- *The negative/naysayer friend.* This is the person who knows everything about nothing, never takes risks, and never has a hard time finding something to complain about. This is also the person who always volunteers his or her opinion and feeds you more information than you can handle (or than you think you can handle). This person will disconnect with you once great things start happening to you.

- *The boundary-less friend.* This is the friend who does not understand her place when she is around your man. She wears overly sexy clothes when she visits, and she grins and smiles in his face. Please get rid of her quickly, whether she has a man or not.

- *Single friends not considering marriage.* These may be co-workers or friends who overly flirt with you or friends who say disrespectful words about your man. I suggest expressing your concerns first and, if the disrespect does not stop, then keeping your distance from these people. Strive to have marriage-ready friends. If you are surrounded by people who are not getting married by choice, you need another crew of friends. This group includes your "sleep-around" girlfriends, party girlfriends, and jaded girlfriends who think all men are scum.

- *The guy friend* who is always trying to push the boundaries. This is the guy who is always there when you need him, but he is also the guy who you do not really want. He is your backup just in case—the one you keep around to ensure you do not grow old and lonely.

People can be dead weight. When you go through a transition in life, along the way you will realize that the wrong person is occupying the wrong space. You must use the principle of restriction when it comes to both family and friends. The company you keep controls your mind.

I personally learned this the hard way. I found that the more I stayed focused on my goal, the easier it was to identify the naysayers or the non-healthy relationship individuals in my life. One particular woman in my life was very logical, well-rounded, experienced in life and career, educated, older, and wiser than me. As a matter of fact, I would be remorse not to acknowledge her because this person came through for me in many personal and career areas of my life and made so many decisions easy and practical for me. Because of this, I thought she would be the right person to help me understand the value in my now-husband. Her advice while I was in my paradigm-preserving mentality was great and it kept me grounded, so I could always identify with her advice and thoughts.

However, as I began to transition and as my transition brought the right man into my life, I eventually understood that I could no longer rely on the advice of this well-respected mentor. Because we were attached at the hip, I called her for almost everything and often spoke to her at least once a week. However, after about a year into my transition, I began to see that her paradigm-preserving ways did not align with my paradigm-modifying goals. Now I am married, but I would not be if I did not make a bold decision to avoid discussing relationship matters with her. If necessary, hopefully your mindset will reveal such individuals a lot sooner. Keep your eyes opened to false teachings.

Thoughts to Ponder

Who are some of the positive people who you want to get and keep in your inner circle?

Who are some of the people in your inner circle, or in your life in general, who you may need to release because of their anti-relationship or anti-marriage thoughts and behaviors?

Be honest, do you maintain a "just in case" relationship with someone? What do you need to do to end that relationship?

Section Four

I am From Missouri, the Show-Me State

Perhaps you are wondering why you should go through this process—what would you gain? If I knew you personally, I could take you by the hand and show you many successful and happy marriages. We could travel from home to home unseen like the spirits in Charles Dickens' *A Christmas Carol*; together we would witness many women who are happy to be wives with their happy husbands. We could peer into marriages and relationships from different cultures and practices that I have seen across the world. We could peek into the lives of over a dozen married women who have gone through the fire and back in their marriages yet remain happy and enjoy being married. As we share this space together, consider this book my opportunity to have this moment with you and let me tell you why I believe you should go through this process.

You should go through this process because there is a bigger destiny for you and bigger fish for you to fry. If you are a leader in your home, family, or in your career, there is a lot at stake because, as leaders, we need to model good behavior. Why should your family and friends doubt your ability to be successful in your career and marriage? Do you want your obituary to speak only about the success of your career and not your success at being married? Sadly, society downplays the role of an effective woman who is also a wife and, in far too many instances, families have suffered for it.

If you are a parent, you are definitely a leader for your children and you must model good behavior for them to follow. Do not allow your children to see their parents living in a system that has no sense of direction, foundation, or structure. Teach your children from the start how to properly conduct themselves in a courtship and prove it with how you conduct yourself. How can you tell your daughter to be chaste when you present her with a bevy of "uncles" with whom you involve yourself? How can you teach your son to respect women when your relationships are ripe with disrespect? Boys should witness what it takes to be a good husband and girls should see what it takes to be a good wife. Notice I did not say a lover, a boo, a booty call, or my dog, but a husband and a wife. This teaches our children to value a serious, responsible, mature, and committed relationship. If you do not have children, then inspire others, such as your siblings, cousins, parents, and friends to do the right thing within their relationships. Not all leaders have the same opportunities; however, every leader, regardless of opportunities and economic resources, has the ability to tap into their resources and work intentionally to set an example.

Thoughts to Ponder

When you have looked in on other marriages, what were some things that impressed you?

What do you believe your life teaches your children about relationships and marriage?

How to Behave During the Paradigm Shift (aka "The Wilderness")

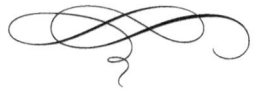

By the time you reach this stage and complete it, you will look brand new. You may resemble Cinderella, the belle of the ball, who is wearing glass slippers and who is far removed from the patched up and torn rags of a woman in turmoil. You will know your shift has brought you out of the wilderness when people start texting and Tweeting you in what seems to be an all-out attack against you, using words purposely designed to crush your spirit. The farther you come out of "the wilderness," the closer you will get to your happiness and the more you may be attacked. I do not want this to be a melancholy message, but there will be times when you will feel like you are alone. You will experience moments where no one understands as you try to get support or explain what you are progressing through. When that time comes, remember to come back and re-read this section of the book. This will not be an "I-told-you-so" moment, or a time to get upset with anyone because the goal to transform is yours alone. Stay focused and treat others kindly; when your sun begins to shine, they will see a brand new you and experience the resulting benefits.

I simply want you to understand that your paradigm shift can feel like a wilderness—a place you may visit but definitely do not want to live in. Let me explain through a childhood memory. When I was young (I guess I was a third-grader at the time), I repeatedly crossed the street from my grandmother's house into a pecan field. I began to skip, hop, and enjoy searching for pecans until I realized I had gone too far into an area of the woods. Despite the fact that it happened multiple times, this was quite frightening to me. I would run in various directions, hoping I would be able to see grandma's house again. Because I was there all by myself, I ran for dear life but would eventually reach my destination unharmed, telling myself that I would never, ever wander off again.

During your paradigm shift, think of the wilderness as an in-between place, meaning you do not relax and make yourself at home there but survey the land and the lessons learned there until you reach your final destination. Wilderness can be a great place to be as long as you realize you are in the wilderness and that you will eventually get through it. I remember one time it took me so long to return from the pecan field to grandma's house that my uncles had to come and find me. While you are in the wilderness, look for others who are in the wilderness or those trying to help you get out of the wilderness, and learn from their best practices and mistakes. If some of your friends are comfortable in the wilderness, leave them there; it works for them. Perhaps when you have moved on, they will follow your example and seek your wisdom.

As I began to learn more about the wifely process, I would joke that a bride should not get married in a wedding dress but in military gear. Wives looked puzzled whenever I made this joke, probably wondering why a happy bride would make such a statement. My self-discovery gave me the wisdom to see that I was preparing to commit to a lifetime of happiness. I prepared myself to live up to the challenge of sustaining my second marriage. In fact, I prepared right up to our wedding day, for I surely was not prepared for my first marriage, and I chose to enter into this new covenant with my paradigm shifted.

If you think getting a husband is hard, I submit that maintaining and sustaining a husband is much more difficult, even during the honeymoon phase. Many times we are not prepared to have a husband. We can get a husband, but we may not be able to keep him if we are not willing to prepare ourselves. One of the worst things that can happen is being blessed to become a wife yet being underprepared to live in a marriage and keep it alive under all conditions. Now I focus on being a good wife, mother, professor, friend, family member, and Christian. I try to rise higher in not only being a wife but in being holistically great in many areas, especially now that I am wiser and more understanding of the power of sacrifice and humbleness as it relates to preparation for the context of being a wife.

So what if you continuously attract the wrong men in your life, make many mistakes, or have a list of other concerns from your past? Just remember you can never have the present without the past. Take advantage of what your past has taught you. Learn from your mistakes. You are the CEO of "You, Inc." and there are many things about you that you need to figure out and resolve within yourself. You cannot rely on people to tell you everything you need to know about you.

Vices (bad habits) will keep you in your wilderness. If you have issues with anger, for example, deal with the obsession of anguish while continuing to maintain your focus. Curb your fixation on overspending on things, such as shoes, clothes, hair, and nails as you continue to learn and remain centered. Whatever vices you have, be they pride, intolerance, stubbornness, clinginess, or the like, work on removing or minimizing them.

Clear your life of bad habits. Stop exposing yourself to negative environments. Bad habits will keep you in the wilderness. Remember that I always entered the pecan wilderness at the same spot, even around the same time of day, and allowed my bad habit of not leaving an audit trail or entering without my parents' permission lead to the same outcome. Clear your head of unnecessary thoughts. Everything that pops up does not need to be taken into consideration. Only consider those thoughts that are aligned with your destiny. I recall that, at the time, my goal was to fill my bag with pecans; I always thought I could have more pecans if I searched further into the trees, never realizing that I could fill my bag from the surrounding four or five trees near the curbside in direct view of grandma's house.

Clear your head of unproductive thoughts, such as hatred or regret. I say this particularly to women who have wounds from past relationships. It is completely unproductive to sit around regretting what has happened in the past. All experiences, mistakes, and missteps can collectively be converted into positive energy so that you might triumph, but often unproductive thoughts develop into excuses and excessive negative energy. You can never be great at anything if you have too many unproductive thoughts. Unproductive thoughts zap your energy, so trash them immediately.

Try not to be too hard on yourself or begin to feel sorry for yourself while you are in the wilderness. Embrace your life as it is—the good and the bad. Empty your head of unforgiving thoughts about yourself and others and practice replacing them with positive, more productive thoughts.

There were times when I lacked confidence in cooking, leading to thoughts that my fiancé was too picky of an eater and that he would complain about my cooking. I would then find myself giving these negative thoughts energy, which showed in how I prepared and introduced the food. I began to forget ingredients and I would add disclaimers like "Babe, feel free to add more salt or other seasonings you like" or "I think I cooked the rice too long" as he prepared his plate. I knew that my insecurities about my cooking drove these statements. The way I think about cooking has changed; I know I am a good cook, and my husband and family enjoy whatever I cook, so I serve it with joy. Now that I have changed how I feel about my ability to cook for my husband, I must admit that I always receive positive feedback.

Take the time to release haters who do not truly support you while you are in the wilderness. Haters and perpetrators will hurt you, so let them go. These individuals envy you and dislike you or your actions for no apparent reason. Haters compel you to consume, or become consistent, in feeding you more negative attitudes than positive ones. In the wilderness, it is not your goal to seek answers as to the motivation and reasoning of these haters but to simply forgive and forget them. Perhaps you will revisit them later but not until you have come full circle with yourself as an individual and have attended to the aspects of yourself that need changing.

Clear your head of unsolicited thoughts, such as the worries and concerns others feel compelled to share with you. Their problems, perceptions, and thoughts are not yours. Avoid asking others about what is going on in their lives if their worries will become the center of your attention and take you off course. You should never mind someone else's business more than you tend to your own.

Make a vow to pursue getting out of the wilderness of being non-wifely with all of your might. Just like you vowed to pursue a career, job, or degree, it is important that you pursue being a wife. Be guilty of pursuing wifely behavior at all cost.

Dedicate time to yourself. The truth is that a man will be fine without you, so you need to focus specifically on you, allowing plenty of room for things that you find inspirational and motivational. Everything you do needs to be about reaching your destination. If your life is too busy for you to focus on yourself, perhaps try committing a mere thirty minutes a week to yourself. Maybe read other books on relationships. My "sacrificial" moments are my bubble bath moments when I read self-help books.

Give what you are trying to accomplish by demonstrating to and helping others. During your growth, talk to others and give them insight on what you have learned through practice, reading, or observation. Just as practice makes perfect, reiteration of the concept from you makes it stick. However, be cautious with whom you share your insight; save it for those who are willing to listen and understand your path.

Separate yourself from others, both enemies and friends (perhaps even your best friend), while you are in the wilderness. The sooner you distinguish between those who want more for you and those who enjoy watching you in the wilderness, the better. Keep in mind that there is a fine line that you must mindfully walk when balancing your need to engage with and your need to separate from others.

As you do all of this, celebrate your way out of the wilderness. The wilderness is rough; you go to bed and do not want to get up, and you have moments of wanting to give up and throw in the towel. It is in these moments that you must start celebrating. Celebrate, somehow, in the midst of the difficultly; do not wait until the victory of getting out of the wilderness. If you can celebrate in difficult times, then you understand that the sun will soon shine on you. When folks frown at you, smile at them. When folks slam the door on you, know that another door will open.

Thoughts to Ponder

Describe your wilderness.

What is your plan to navigate through and out of the wilderness?

Section Five

From the Wilderness to Being Even More Transparent

Introduction

How are you feeling so far in this process? I believe that you are well on your way to releasing the wifely characteristics that live deep inside of you. Soon, you will be a great combination of a successful career woman, great wife, wonderful mother, and good friend/family member.

However, there remain shrubs within your wilderness. Moving through and out of the wilderness will cause you to ask why it feels as though you are losing or giving up so much of what you believe in. It also creates some anxiety about how to translate all of that into a conversation with the potential husband who has extended his hand and heart. Be strong; there is advice.

What Do I Have to Sacrifice?

Being a wife is bigger than your current skill set, training, and experience. Preparation for it entails sacrificing your current mindset. You need a desire and commitment to sacrifice because you may have to sacrifice a lot. Remember that greatness cannot be achieved without sacrifice. My life is full of sacrifices, such as quitting my job, relocating my family, and downsizing from a house to a two-bedroom apartment so I could pursue my Ph.D. and support my entire family on scholarships. I also sacrificed watching TV and other me-time activities. My life is the result of the great accomplishments that came from those great sacrifices. Just like academic excellence requires sacrifice, so does becoming a wife. No one comes out of the womb understanding what it takes to be a good wife.

This process may cost you an arm and a leg, given the deep-rooted nature of your strongholds, beliefs, and behaviors. If you are in the same mental place I was when I decided to shift, it will not cost you anything but the willingness to endure some pain, a positive outlook, and a walk in faith. The process of becoming wifely material was enjoyable in totality but not always in its parts.

The process of preparing to be a wife will undoubtedly require you to delete individuals from your favorite five, your speed dial, and social networking sites. This process will require you to take a hard and honest look in the mirror and remind you that you are beautiful and deserve a husband.

First, you have to detoxify yourself. This means eliminating conversations that linger in your mind, seep through your pores, and pour out of your mouth that are self-defeating, inaccurate, false, non-ladylike, and/or vulgar. The process of being seen as a virtuous wife will require you to walk a new walk and talk a new talk. You must become a person who can be admired, honored, and respected as a wife. No ladies, he is not lucky to have you as the paradigm-preserving mindset would have you to believe; you are lucky to have him.

You will come to understand and believe that trials and errors have a purpose because injury and recovery is a wilderness place where one learns PERSEVERANCE 101. Each time you adjust an old way of thinking, you will be challenged by the manifestation of the new way of thinking.

You will have to push back those who are still in the old mindset and exhibit behaviors that you once promoted. The bad girls and corporate divas clubs are probably going to revoke your membership when you start talking about going home to focus on the things that will prepare you to be a wife or a better wife. So be it! Move toward your vision, understanding that what you see for you often has nothing to do with what others see for themselves. Remember, nothing ventured, nothing gained. What could be so wrong with venturing deeper into your psyche and making some adjustments in order to gain a love that you have prepared yourself for?

Here is a very short list of the most prominent issues that will thwart your progress in becoming wifely material: anger, impatience, jealously, low self-esteem, gossiping, being too talkative, being a busy body, laziness, negativity, over-spending and impulsive spending, the need for immediate and constant gratification, being attention-seeking, lack of focus, extreme independence, over-thinking everything, pride, lack of leadership, lack of commitment, inability to let things go, sex-appeal overload, hyper-sensitivity, an inability to humble yourself, and believing you are not the problem. Hallelujah! Breathe. If you are not willing to admit your weaknesses, ask a handful of trusted co-workers, relatives, and friends to point them out for you. If you listen, they can help you identify your challenge areas fairly quickly. Take the compiled list based on their observations and begin to rid yourself of them. It may help if you follow my example; I posted my challenge issues list on my bedroom wall so that I could be constantly reminded of what I needed to work through. You should also release them to God and ask Him to purge you of them. Happily, I can now say my prayers were answered.

Thoughts to Ponder

Make a list of things that you have sacrificed to reach your goals.

Have you ever regretted making sacrifices?

What are your challenge issues? What have you done to overcome these issues?

Where Do I Start?

Start now, right where you are. Know that your transformation will not happen overnight. Being wifely material *should* come naturally, with so much joy and excitement. A natural response to your husband requires a shifting of your mindset, a relinquishing of the boardroom-control mentality at home and the respect of your husband in his position. You also want to try to be well-rounded and cater to your man. As a well-rounded woman, you are caring, understanding, intelligent, nurturing, respectful, and beautiful inside and out. You are physically appealing and able to relate to a myriad of people. You have the skills you need in a marriage: being able to cook a meal, knowing when to turn on/off the aggression, and knowing when to be wonderfully permissive and submissive. If you desire to be a wife, being well-rounded is appreciating all aspects of life, knowing that your knowledge is limited. You surround yourself with positive women and wives who can delicately help you overcome the limitations. And yes, part of being well-rounded means you know it is okay, even sexy, to cater to your man. You want to be in a mental and emotional place where your catering to him comes without the famous "it has to be fifty-fifty" discussion, a line of complaints, or your laundry list of things you do and do not do.

This is not to say that you should have a slave mentality but that we do all things that come naturally to us easily and enjoyably, which in turn creates a positive and loving environment. If you love to dance, no one has to ask you to dance when your favorite song comes on. You simply start snapping your fingers and start dancing. The same is true for those who naturally cook.

A natural cook can whip up a four-course meal with limited items in the refrigerator, while most of us would turn to a cookbook and purchase many one-time-use ingredients. During your transition, feel great about getting to the state of naturally being every woman that your husband needs. Everyone likes to be near someone who has positive, catering behaviors—naturally.

Thoughts to Ponder

Do you have a desire for wife-like behaviors to come naturally? If so, what has stopped you from acting naturally in this capacity?

If you were a man, what would your ideal wife be like? Could you be her?

But I Fear Exposing the Real Me

Believe me, I understand how difficult it is to take as little as one moment to examine one's self. Personal experience teaches that looking in the mirror can be a scary yet bold and positive move, particularly if you are ready to grow. If you are like most of us, your automatic answer of "Okay" to the question "How are you?" may be a sign that you are maladjusted, or not willing or afraid to share that you are silently in pain. Secret suffering, whether it is because of finances, a broken relationship, or a plethora of other life issues, has no great value and does not help us grow, particularly when no one else knows what is going on in our lives. When you share your insecurities and fears (or at least admit them to yourself), the private walls that hold you back begin to slowly break down.

Besides, people take note of your shortcomings anyway, and they can tell when you have not discovered important aspects of life and love. Life is about learning how to give and receive love. With this in mind, it would benefit you to share your challenges and struggles with your closest friends. Praying helps as well.

If you want something different from a relationship, remove the armor. Removing the armor will expand your experience of who you really are. You will become more transparent to yourself and others. I ask that as you read forward, you let this be the last day you wear your armor. Do not hang it in your closet or donate it to charity because no one else needs your armor either! Tell the armor what you have told men in your life: "Go and don't come back!"

Any time you are close to someone, you run the risk of being betrayed, just as they run the risk of you betraying them. Betrayal is an inside job; in other words, strangers do not betray us. Nearly every person you encounter has been betrayed in a relationship, and there is nothing unique about being hurt or being lied to. The problem comes when the protective armor you develop as a result of your wounds makes it difficult for others to get at your core substance. You should work on experiencing true healing to avoid the pitfall of forcing others to pay retribution for something they did not do or to work through your discomfort and trust issues. The bigger picture is you cannot be patched but have to be healed and made whole. So peeling away the layers or removing the armor reveals the better part of you. Without healing, the peeling may reveal the fractured, numb, and hurt side of you, but this does not mean you should go through life concealing the better part of you. How do you want to live your life—revealing the best part of you or concealing the best part of you? To be able to deal with your pain and become totally healed of it may require professional counseling, therapy, or spiritual guidance.

You would not like being the recipient of your man's concealment of pain, hurt, and fears (e.g., "Baby, I love you. I just cannot trust you because of what I went through before.") As a woman, the last thing you want to experience with a man you want to build a future with is having to peel away all the layers that he has in order to advance with him. I believe it is always easier for you to understand the effect of concealing rather than revealing. I understand layers; I know how they happen. I do understand that when you are hurt you do not want to be hurt the same way again. The armor you create covers you and you become comfortable in it. Yet, when you wear that armor, how can your eyes illuminate joy and peace? What freedom exists in your life? Can true joy exist in your life when you are walking around concealed? Take the steps to reveal yourself and be confident in who you are—healed from your hurt.

Thoughts to Ponder

Do you understand your layers and how they were formed?

How do your layers impact how you interact with others?

What do you have to lose if you reveal yourself?

How would revealing yourself make you feel?

Have you healed from your past? Have you forgiven yourself? Do you love yourself?

Does pride ever get in your way? Please explain.

Does fear ever get in your way? Please explain.

Section Five

Your Cry for Help

In her song "Baggage," Mary J. Blige sings lyrics that I related to. The song was meaningful to me because I knew I acted out unfavorable/bad behaviors in my relationships that did not align with my destiny. These behaviors were the result of first and secondhand physical, emotional, mental, and spiritual experiences that helped me understand right from wrong, kind from unkind, and warm versus cold behavior. Yet, I continued to act in such an unhealthy manner despite this knowledge. I could not get my actions to align with what I knew to be kind, gentle, and respectful behavior toward a man. After all, during this time in my life, I did not perceive my behavior to be all that bad, particularly given that no one was complaining and everyone was still reinforcing the notion that I was a great catch. Thus, I made excuses, focused on other things that I thought mattered, and applauded myself for acknowledging that all was not great with me. This was my cry for help. I would not be surprised if your cry sounded very much the same: baggage, followed by cycles that led to more baggage, manifesting in interior and exterior reinforcement that led back to the baggage.

"Baggage" is about a woman admitting she is aware that she is acting in unloving ways. She is indirectly asking for help and stating she does not know how to fix her damaging behaviors at the moment. The lyrics also indicate her understanding that she should not continue down the same path—a path that a man does not deserve. She is crying out for help. When you are at this stage, you must be willing to do more than sing the song; you must boldly confess to someone and ask for guidance to pull you through.

As a woman, you have moments of awareness of your unfavorable actions but have not embarked on the breakthrough that is needed for change. Our weaknesses and insecurities are often regulated by self-protective acts and manifest through our wish list of what we expect of a man. We progress toward the paradigm shift once we acknowledge that change is necessary and begin to transition in such a way that our behavior reflects our efforts in growth. The paradigm-modifying mindset stage is more of a continuous, proactive behavior where you understand the old you and make constant efforts to align your mindset, and thus your behavior, with the growing you. You are attempting to advance and get closer to graduation in the paradigm-modifying mindset. Recognize your cry for help and if you have to, cry on the shoulder of someone who respects and understands where you are and whose mindset is positioned to nurture you toward the edge of the wilderness.

Thoughts to Ponder

Have you recognized your cry for help? If so, what is it? If not, can you admit that you may be ignoring it?

Baggage is something many people take into new relationships. What do you think is in the baggage you are carrying?

What can you do today to productively address your baggage and/or cry for help?

Have you shared your baggage with anyone?

Remain Focused Throughout the Process

Focusing is the necessary process for advancement to the paradigm-modified mindset. Functioning in a disorderly manner will not advance you to this state. We often fail to let ourselves and others see the true, purified, pre-scorned us because of our lack of focus in this area. Staying focused will help you to advance through the paradigm shift from a paradigm-preserving mindset to a paradigm-modified mindset. Paradigm shifting is analogous to the wilderness. If you stay focused on getting out of the wilderness, you will learn, modify, and advance, eventually finding your way out. The wilderness is not a place you want to remain, especially given that you know there is a place you are trying to reach—the natural state of being a wife. Your journey is a prerequisite to being marriage material.

What Can I Do About My Toughest Moments in the Wilderness?

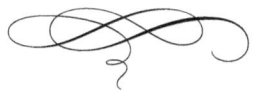

Anticipate and prepare for those toughest moments like they are part of a thrilling adventure. While in the wilderness, you must want to get out and stay out. No one accidentally gets out of the wilderness. There are individuals in your life who are relying on you to make the transition. Thus, submit yourself to the process of moving. You must submit to the process even when you cannot receive or see the immediate benefit.

Even when you get out of the wilderness, there will be times that you will wander back. However, the next time around, assuming you are within the paradigm-modifying mindset, you will be better positioned to find your way out. The reason many frequently return to the wilderness is because they do not have a plan, and they lack determination and focus.

Your time in the wilderness will be trying as we all have patches of thin skin on our bodies that are unmanageable. So, while in the wilderness, become well aware of your thin spots and rejoice in experiences that make your thin spots thicker. Our thin spots are typically tied to our insecurities. When we release insecurities and detach ourselves from prior bad experiences, we become more accepting of who we are as individuals and thus can focus on who we need to become moving forward. When you fail to release your insecurities, these thin areas of your mind will prevent you from sharing, seeking, and growing, resulting in a stagnant life. Do not spend a significant amount of your time protecting yourself when the willingness to release fears would take you further in life.

People are aware of our thin-skinned areas and will attack the same spot over and over again, expecting us to react the same way every time. These thin areas are the toughest to protect in the wilderness. Focus on securing the thin areas of your mind so that when the enemy attacks you are less likely to respond in a negative manner. Allow your experiences in the wilderness to perfect you or to help someone see your transition. Believe me, you will know when you are progressing. All will see how differently you respond to situations. Over time, you will become oblivious to the attacks and will have a built-in strength that protects you and allows you to feel relaxed and mature.

Thoughts to Ponder

What opportunities have you had to practice within your most trying moments?

Do you and others witness improvements in your behavior?

Section Five

Finally, a Road Map to Guide Me Into Becoming Marriage Material

I discuss having a roadmap for success not only for transitioning from the paradigm-modifying mindset but also for remaining within your modified mindset. In this chapter, I provide you with a roadmap that allows you to guide your conduct while in courtship. Moving away from this roadmap should cause you anxiety and place you in a position to rationalize and justify a detour. We do not want to get into rationalizing or detouring when our target is so clear, do we? What is our target? To become a wonderful wife who is a blessing to her husband. So let's take a look at some universal street signs you need to be aware of in order to make courtship decisions based on your roadmap. Keep in mind that you can travel at different speeds and by different methods (e.g., car, walk, bus, train, and bike).

Your Own Street Sign. Imagine having a street sign with your name on it. Establish your own vision of a highway and take charge of who is allowed to enter your street from the highway. Know that while you cannot control the highway, you surely have a lot of control over traffic on your street. Your street should have many street signs (rules) about how you process information. Your street will need maintenance work at times, and your signs may need revising. For the purpose of your transition, your street is there to guide you to developing wifely behavior. Assuming that you have the correct signs and your street receives regular maintenance, deviating from your street's rules should cause conflict with your desire to one day be a wife.

You also have the choice of deciding how many entry points and exit points exist on your street along with what types of street signs are on it. Let's visit a few street signs you may consider for your road, particularly given there is a highway surrounding you that you cannot control.

Curves and Corners. These signs signal that there is danger ahead caused by unexpected or sharp curves and turns. Signs may also come in the form of a SLIPPERY WHEN WET warning or ROUGH ROAD AHEAD sign. Within your journey, you will experience unexpected curves and dangerous territories on the road.

I remember traveling on a dark road once, not really knowing what lay ahead. I started thinking of all the possibilities, such as a dangerous hitchhiker or a deer running out in front of the car. I was nervous and reviewed what I could do to stay calm and ensure that I remained on the road, no matter how sharp the curve. I also remember driving slower than normal since I was unfamiliar with the road.

The same thing will happen to you when your journey appears dark and all you have is a small beam of hope. Allow that beam to keep you moving forward, as you know the road will end eventually. There are situations that you will come across, and you need to recognize that you are unfamiliar with them, so drive slowly and cautiously, taking calculated steps. In this same category, we have the SLIPPERY WHEN WET sign. This sign should be a signal to you and others that you are not your best when it comes to this area of your street. Explain to individuals that this portion is still under construction and that everyone must exercise caution until travel on that section of the street is permissible.

Merge Signs. There are various types of merge signs: some allow you to merge with traffic while others direct you to merge to the left or to the right. With the merge sign, you need to know when you should enter traffic and when you should look for the nearest exit.

I remember having a conversation with my mom and asking her why I would not just leave when I was in an uncomfortable environment. I had been invited to a going-away party for a friend. At the time I was engaged and found myself surrounded by unhappily married, divorced, and single women. After drinking a few glasses of wine, these women began to focus on me and explain how my excitement of being married would be short-lived. While I was more than capable of handling this conversation, I was unhappy about my ability to know when to exit from it. After all, if I was paying attention while driving, the signs were clear when I started out on this highway, and they became clearer as I continued to travel (in this case, staying engaged in the conversation).

In other words, there will be times when you need to figure out when to merge with traffic while moving toward the nearest exit. Do not pass this exit or get off at the next one. Get off at that first exit quickly. Other times you need to master merging into traffic. I think of my positive friends and my network of great folks who are leaders. I am glad that I mastered the art of merging with the right crowd. An old supervisor of mine asked me when I was in my early twenties, "Why do you hang with people who cannot do anything for you?" At the time, I was shocked at the question and believed he was unjustified in making this statement. This question came from a well-educated people-person and high-profile individual. In hindsight, I see he had a valid point. We all need to surround ourselves with individuals who add value to our lives instead of those individuals who block us from those who could enhance our lives.

DO NOT ENTER. A DO NOT ENTER sign means that you cannot proceed in that direction, or you may be headed the wrong way. Something is happening in that area and you are not allowed to enter. Avoid these areas at all costs. These signs may also come in the form of a STOP or DON'T WALK indicator. In any case, stay clear of these areas or risk jeopardizing all that you have worked so hard to obtain.

I believe there are various DO NOT ENTER signs in our lives that women should stay clear of. One of these is to never engage in a ménage-a-trois. I have heard stories of women who have been asked to engage in such relationships. This is a danger zone and you should stay clear. Other danger zones are self-doubt, self-hate, and hatred of others. Stay clear of negative language and behavior toward men. Telling a man you do not need him, being condescending, or acting too overbearing are all negative areas. Can you image someone telling you that they do not need you? Never make a man feel less than you. If you have ever heard a man say the words "I just do not feel like I am good enough for you" or "You make me feel like you are better than me," then you have obviously entered into the DO NOT

ENTER zone. A courtship is not a place to toot your own horn. Never say anything bad about his family, including his mother. Even if he asks your opinion, simply take the lighter road and suggest that he give it some thought. Stay free and clear of this dialogue. Become more of a listener than a commentator, a referee, or a coach. DO NOT ENTER into having a foul mouth. At times I hear women using offensive language and wonder if they know any other words.

One Way. There are street signs that let you know that traffic is moving in one direction. When you are on this street, the only way to go back is by doing a U-turn. There are times in your life when you should allow yourself to travel in only one direction. I remember working really hard to modify the way I conducted myself in relationships by changing my tone and my behavior, so there was no way that I wanted to use the U-turn option, since I understood I was making a change for the better. Thus, within your life, there must be portions of your road that can only go ONE WAY.

Passing Lane. Ever been driving and had the urge to pass another vehicle so you could travel at a faster speed? You will have to treat some areas in your life this way.

In the past, I always believed that my time was valuable and that I was a genuinely great person. So, if you underestimated my value and my contributions or took them for granted, I would grow angry. Once the anger boiled over, I would think about how much I sacrificed (e.g., my work, friends, me, family) and adopt the "How could you?" attitude. I can laugh at this scenario now because I no longer think this way. I now know that we all fall short of others' expectations and that we are only in control of our own feelings and behaviors. The vehicle I needed to pass was not someone else's but my own portion of me that would get angry at huge disappointments. I needed to leave this portion of my thought process behind. Thus, it was imperative that I passed this "THING" and moved quickly ahead, separating myself as much as possible from my old thoughts and behaviors. Do you have anything within yourself that is a slow-moving vehicle that you simply need to pass quickly?

STOP. The STOP sign should cause you to pause for a few seconds to analyze the situation. Typically, we have to observe and understand our surroundings before we can proceed. There are times in your journey when you need to STOP and not rush to judge or to speak but simply STOP and observe.

This area is not necessarily a danger zone. My husband does not know this, but there are times when I have an opinion or think I know the answer, but I practice STOPPING and observing the situation. In these situations, using the STOP sign allows me to observe my husband in full leadership mode. Through the process of STOPPING and watching him proceed, I learn that there are decisions I do not need to make—decisions he can make better—and that I am not right about everything. You will find situations that will require you to STOP before proceeding. As you proceed, you may find that you have to follow, lead, or do absolutely nothing.

U-Turn. There are times when I am grateful for the U-TURN sign. The U-TURN allows us to reverse our direction of travel. Where there are many scenarios that call for this sign, I immediately think of the times when I have traveled in the wrong direction for a distance. I have a choice to continue in the wrong direction or make a U-turn. For me, this is typically my apology area or my desire to retry an approach. I admit that I am not always my best person, but my humbleness allows me to go back to the drawing board and take that opportunity to make it better.

During my transition, I used the U-turn option quite often.

Yield. Personally, I love the YIELD sign. It brings me joy. A yield sign typically means to slow down and prepare to stop. When I am exercising my yield, I can feel myself in the moment of caution. This means that I am analyzing and will avoid experiencing any unexpected events. Additionally, I prepare to make a number of potential choices. There are times when your antennas should be fully alert and the moments within the current event are salient.

Thoughts to Ponder

What are the street signs within your neighborhood?

How would your life change if you governed your streets?

What daily reminders will you use to keep yourself focused and from going off track?

What are your SLIPPERY WHEN WET areas?

What areas of your life do you need to hold up a DO NOT ENTER sign?

How do you recognize when you are approaching a curvy or slippery road? How do you typically react?

Is there anyone in your life who you would like to pass in the passing lane?

What Should I Expect From Others During My Transition?

If you are a divorced or single parent on the path to becoming wifely material, you may definitely find that your transition to welcome this extremely important person into your life will upset your children and/or your ex-spouse. When it comes to your children, their cautious reaction is natural; after all, they have always been your focus and have seen you go through various relationships. If the children are older, they also probably think they know what is best for you, them, and mankind. This could also apply to anyone who depends on you to be there for them 24/7, such as your parents, girlfriends, or co-workers. They will be rightfully hurt but will heal with time. Eventually they will appreciate your transition. You may be the first to transition only to then sit back and watch them leap in your direction.

If you are currently in a relationship, your man may not to be receptive to your change. After all, he may have never had a woman like the woman you are about to become and may feel lost and confused during the process. He may be used to being treated a certain way and become insecure, or he may welcome the change. Regardless of your man's reaction, if you are changing for the better, keep moving forward.

Your transition will not occur overnight. At a minimum, it will take a few years, especially given that you are trying to re-program old thoughts and behaviors while fighting off the enemy that will come in every form and from every direction. Overall, you will struggle with yourself and those closest to you. Change will occur and the road may be rough, but happiness is sure to follow. If the transition was an easy process, we would all be married and the U.S. Census Bureau statistics would be different.

When Do I Apologize?

While in the wilderness, you will make mistakes, so you must practice the skill of apologizing. Apologizing does not come easy to everyone, however. These are questions that you can ask yourself when deciding if you should apologize: Did I hurt this person's feelings—at least from their perspective? What did I do? Could I have done it better? What did I say? Could I have said it better? If your response to any one of these questions is yes, then you should apologize.

Thoughts to Ponder

What are your thin layers/areas? In other words, what subjects really get you fired up?

Who needs an apology from you?

Section Five

Transition Like a Backstroke

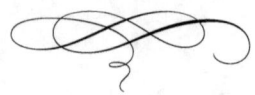

Many times, problems are repetitive in nature. They have the tendency to recur, and all you can do is stay above water and tackle them the best way you know how. From this day forward, instead of trying to stay above water, do your best to backstroke into peace regarding matters related to your transition to be a wife. I promise you that things will look brighter on the other side and that what you classify as a problem today will eventually disappear. Why did I say backstroke? When I took swimming lessons, the trainer taught us many swimming techniques, but the only ones that I enjoyed and could master with ease were floating and the backstroke. As the instructor taught us how to float, he repeatedly reminded us to relax. I could not float until I became calm, patient, carefree, and methodical. Once I learned how to float, I learned how to do the backstroke. It was amazing how I could be positioned partially above water, look up at the sky, isolate folks around me, and relax at the same time—all while swimming the backstroke. In my mind, the backstroke was all I needed to avoid drowning because it would maneuver me out of trouble's way.

A no-holds-barred paradigm shift will allow you to accomplish this backstroke. In order to shift, you have to equip yourself with the resources and knowledge to begin your journey of change. Remember, change is good! To successfully progress from paradigm-preserving to paradigm-modifying, make the choice to solely focus on ways to improve yourself and to take responsibility for all your past and present actions. When you have a combination of the desire to improve, focus, and take ownership of all your life journeys (good and bad) and have expectations of a miraculous outcome, the backstroke is possible.

Most individuals have a tendency to see things through the lens of scarcity; all they see is life and all its problems. You do not have to attend a workshop to develop these "woe is life" skills. You can fill a boardroom with individuals who know all the problems but offer no solutions. When it comes to marriage, you look in your rear-view mirror at past relationships and think that marriage equates to inevitable trouble. Regarding negative thoughts pertaining to marriage, I encourage you to disregard what it looks like and what it sounds like during the beginning of your transition. Do not look at what you can see since vision is very limited. As an unmarried woman, you lack the vision, capacity, and knowledge that are only gained through marriage. If you decide to take a peek at what it can be, think about the potential in you to prepare yourself for the journey rather than thinking of marriage as full of problems.

Thoughts to Ponder

What is your potential to prepare yourself for the marriage journey?

What kind of leadership skills do you think a spouse should have in marriage?

How Do I Get Out of The Wilderness?

Keep in mind that if you are going to get out of the wilderness and be victorious, you need a strategic plan. All successful companies have a mission statement accompanied by a strategic goal, process, and full plan with details. You are going to have so many distractions and hurdles trying to keep you from engaging in a better life. Consequently, you have to take the same winning approach that you have used in other areas of your life to be successful. Map it out, develop short-term goals and objectives, create a vision board, write your marriage mission statement, and follow your process sheet. It is extremely important that you protect your focus and that you take it seriously. Personal growth is a benefit of your plan, but becoming wifely material is your target—the center of your focus. Many individuals will see your target as clearly as you do and will, at some point, even attempt to block you from reaching it with tales of marriages that did not last, "what about you" theories, "too much to lose" statements, and other defeating darts. Therefore, be prepared to guard your target against the following:

Guard against anti-marriage behavior. Anti-marriage behavior occurs when you engage in thoughts and activities that give off false indicators that you will not make a good wife. These indicators include stubbornness, materialistic values, non-ladylike behavior, and placing your girls' trips as high priority.

Guard against the loss of your focus. Be prepared for the unknowns that will happen during your transition and cause you to lose focus. This is not a time to let your guard down. Your goals could be compromised the very moment someone finds out that you are losing focus (or have your guard down), but be sure to get back on track.

Guard against the dislikes of marriage preparation material. Some of us just do not like things that promote women practicing wifely behavior, such as being submissive and humble and cooking. Remember the time your parents made you eat your vegetables and you thought you were having one of the worst moments of your life until one day you began to eat vegetables and actually liked them? If you practice liking marriage-preparation materials, no matter how bad they make you feel, you may just discover that you like them and that they are necessary. Stay engaged with your marriage materials until you discover that they are something you cannot live without. You get stronger by reading and listening to pro-marriage material and weaker by staying within the anti-marriage mindset.

Thoughts to Ponder

What is your marriage mission statement?

What types of things do you see on your marriage vision board?

What are some pro-marriage materials you can quickly identify and add to your collection?

Section Five

How Do I Get Out of The Wilderness— There's More?

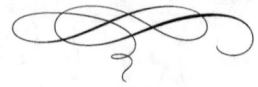

Getting out of the wilderness requires action. Getting out is a learning process—a process that requires diligence, consistency, and study. It is similar to college courses where you have to learn some things on your own. Some things you will not quite get at the moment or see how they are applicable, and you have to ascertain the meaning of other things and how they apply to your life. Additionally, there will be midterm and final exams. Some of you will pass with flying colors and others will ask for permission to re-take the exams.

To get out of the wilderness, you must maintain a high level of excitement and optimism, which allows you to simply ignore many of the doubtful emotions, behaviors, and thoughts of the naysayers that are likely to come your way. Practice isolating yourself from your closest friends and relatives and, at times, your own mind. No matter how difficult the moment is or the obstacle that is thrown your way, you must be determined to do whatever it takes to overcome it and transition into a new paradigm.

To get out of the wilderness, cheerfully accept the responsibility and do your best. You have to do your best because it impacts more than you. If you mishandle this area, you are not just leading yourself astray; you are leading others astray. You are not the only one affected by doing your best to have a healthy relationship; everyone is affected.

Many sports fans declare "Go Big or Go Home" or "Come with your A-game." Perhaps you have heard the saying "Do your best or don't do it at all." If anything great is going to happen in your life, whether socially, relationally, professionally, or academically, it starts with a positive and healthy mindset. A positive mindset means that you are willing to try and feel optimistic about the outcome. Make up your mind that nothing will get in the way of your moving forward. Your mindset must remain strong so that it can speak to mountains, naysayers, haters, doubters, and challenges. Include the idea that failure is not an option in your mindset. You can only rise to the level of your mindset. Your mind must believe that you can excel in a relationship and that you can excel in balancing your life and your responsibilities as a woman in a relationship. Many women have learned to do this and so can you!

To get out of the wilderness, meditate. Meditating is your quiet moment without distraction. It helps you connect with your inner wisdom, gain insight, and focus. Meditate to feed your mind with hope and positive thoughts. Focus your thoughts on a positive outcome, day and night, so that you will be careful to do everything that aligns with your optimistic thoughts. While meditation comes in different forms, meditating for me means taking five minutes to an hour to calibrate. I think about my goal of preparing myself to be a great wife and all that is expected of a great wife, friend, supporter, and more. I also reflect on my thoughts and actions. Whenever anything is misaligned, I analyze that area in an effort to align my future actions to a place that fits within my goal of being wifely material.

To get out of the wilderness, have persistence. If marriage is in your future plans, you must remember that becoming wifely material will require persistence. Achieving and maintaining anything great requires persistence. You must put forth some effort; you must endeavor. Excellence in execution comes from putting effort into your goals. Persistence in reaching your goals starts with having a change in position and the right mindset. Being great wifely material will not happen just by saying it, and most likely it does not come naturally. It is not going to happen through osmosis or by simply reading this and other self-help books. Just like you do when accomplishing other great goals in your life, you will be required to have zealous persistence. You must be willing to grind, which does not mean that you are "in it to win it," but that losing is not an option. Persistence will get you prepared for your appointed season, and then you must model this same persistency and consistency in all of your actions. You are trying to cultivate an atmosphere of not giving up when things get tough, or because you do not understand, or because you are uncomfortable, but instead continue until you accomplish your goal. Demonstrate that being a wife is a learning process and that you will never get to a point or place in your life where you give up and stop learning about how to be a better wife.

Along with persistence, being a great wife must be a priority. In other words, excellence in this area must be a main concern. You must have and display care and effort in pursuing your goals. Showing love must be important, since this area is too vital not to be at the forefront of your existence. If you are going to achieve this goal or any goal, it is only going to be when your priorities are in order. When you evaluate your relationships and try to figure out why things are misaligned, perhaps it is because you have not prioritized correctly. When you prioritize, you get the major factors associated with your goals in order. When you focus and organize your major elements, you achieve positive consistency and predictability.

Thoughts to Ponder

What actions are you willing to take to get out of your wilderness?

What priority will you give your transition to becoming marriage material? Why?

Section Five

Epilogue

Have you ever decided to take a different route in order to arrive at your desired destination? This is the fundamental aspect of this book. When you desire to become a wife and commit yourself to it, you increase the likelihood of becoming a wife. However, you have to be open to exploring a different route in order to end up in a different spot. You must release those paradigm-preserving beliefs and notions and modify your thought processes with a positive, productive, and prosperous vision of what your marriage will be like and how you will perform as a wife. Independent, single women should understand that where they are now is not their final destination. I am sharing what I learned on my journey to becoming a wife in an effort to get you to a place where you will have more than enough to enable you to have a tremendous impact on others.

Exploration reveals the possibility of what can be. You should want to know more and put yourself in a position to be exposed to more in order to expand your imagination. It is no mistake that you are reading this book. There is something bigger and better for you, and I believe you are ready to go get it!

When you go through your seasons of preparation, you must keep your belief system intact. Your focus must be on you but only for the purpose of attracting and maintaining a great man for marriage. Do not be concerned about who talks about you. Be willing to stand for what is rightfully yours. Once you have transitioned, be willing to share what your transformation has done for you.

For the unmarried ladies, no matter where you are on your journey through the matrimonial process, remember that you must push forward. You know what is holding you back because you know yourself better than anyone else. You must move beyond your heart and understand that marriage is for richer or for poorer, in sickness and in health, for better or for worse. If a metamorphosis occurs in either one of you, you will still be together. There is a man in this world who was made specifically for you. When you grow in your behavior and you put the thought of attracting a good man into your life, your wishes are more likely to come true.

For the new wives, I encourage you to recall your wedding day when everyone you loved rejoiced in your marriage. Remember how your wedding made others dance and fall in love all over again. Such memories will help you see your marriage in a positive light. Even after we find a husband, we must strive to be a better wife for him. We must make it so that he feels honored, respected, loved, and nurtured. We must always remain eye candy; never let your eye candy disappear. Being married is not an automatic ticket to happily-ever-after.

For the seasoned wives, take lessons from a newlywed. Do not isolate yourself from newlyweds. In fact, sponsor an "I Love My Husband Positivity Party" where the newlyweds share their secrets with women who have been married for quite some time. Give your husband a new you, a new woman. Make him fall in love with you all over again. If necessary, forgive him for the past and forgive yourself. When he takes you to dinner or to the movies, turn up the sexiness. At times, switch up the roles and do special things for him as well.

No one can make this change and instill motivation in you. You must believe that it is possible, and you must believe that your possibilities increase once you exercise the lessons learned in this book.

Finally, I know that I experienced this journey for both you and me. God knew that you would read this book one day. Although I do not know your future, I know that you can only become a better person, particularly given that this book exists to make you a better you so that Mr. Right will want you in his life and find you fitting to be his wife. It is also written to encourage you to become an example to other women who want to transition to a paradigm- modifying mindset. Looking like marriage material is one of the greatest compliments that you can receive. You are not promised today or tomorrow, so do not hesitate—become the wife exemplified right now.

About the Author

Dr. Smith is a wife, mother, sister, friend, researcher, and professor. From day one, she has always lived with a purpose and a desire to help others. Her positive, motivating, and engaging mindset emanates from her spirit. She was raised in a loving blended family and now has one of her own. Dr. Smith knows what it is like to step outside your comfort zone, rise to new levels in life, and persevere through the challenges. Her humbleness, love for individuals, experiences with all walks of life, transparency, and wisdom allows her to easily connect with individuals.

Dr. Smith received her PhD from the University of South Florida. She also attend the College of William & Mary as well as Christopher Newport University. She has worked for major corporate and government organizations (e.g., Big 4 accounting firm, the CIA, NASA, the Inspector General, and universities). Surviving as a single parent, excelling in her career, and serving the community are all areas of life that came naturally to Dr. Smith. She, however, lacked the desire, growth, and knowledge of understanding the importance of being capable of balancing both a career and a family that includes a husband. Once she gained this wisdom, she was able to unlock the door that kept her blind to the number of advantages to marriage. Most importantly, she unlocked the door that allowed her to grow to a new level.

Dr. Smith's research has been published in premier journals, such as *The Accounting Review*, the *Journal of Information Systems*, *Decision Sciences*, and the *International Journal of Accounting Information Systems*. She is also a speaker, presenting her work worldwide.

She is the recipient of many awards, scholarships, and grants, including Honorary Recipient of the PricewaterhouseCoopers Auditing Alchemy Inc. Grant, the Russell Ewald Award for Academic Excellence and Human Service, the

Institute of Internal Auditors–Michael J. Barrett Doctoral Dissertation Award, The PhD Project, and the Florida Education Fund.

In her first book, *You Are More Than What Meets The Eye: The Independent Woman's Guide to Becoming Wifely Material*, Dr. Smith believes that both women and their husbands (future or current) will benefit. She is from the Hampton Roads area and currently resides in South Florida.

www.ingramcontent.com/pod-product-compliance
Lightning Source LLC
LaVergne TN
LVHW051602070426
835507LV00021B/2713